WHO YOU ARE MEANT TO BE

The Enneagram Effect

ROSEMARY HURWITZ, MA. PS

WHO YOU ARE MEANT TO BE

The Enneagram Effect

Published by
Transcendent Publishing
PO Box 66202
St. Pete Beach, FL 33706
www.transcendentpublishing.com

ISBN: 978-0-9600501-3-0

Printed in the United States of America.

DEDICATION

To my soul mate and husband:

Dale, your disciplined ways and love in action, inspire me to move my enlightened dreams into reality.

And to our beautiful children:

Claire Rose, your commitment to integrity, wholeness, creativity and joy inspires me to my personal best every day.

Christopher Joseph, your openhearted strength inspires me to enjoy loving interdependent relationships, and to feel good setting my own limits.

Carly Marisa, your gentle kind presence inspires me to love and nurture the quiet places where I am content and enough.

Caitlin Rachel, your helpfulness and thoughtfulness along with an ability to own your power inspires me to love my self and others more fully.

And to Kelly Marie, you are the flower that keeps growing within me. In the ways that come with deep loss, you have inspired me to keep opening the doors within. I look so forward to holding you close in heaven, as I have in my heart on earth.

CONTENTS

PREFACE

People have been asking me to write *Who You Are Meant To Be, The Enneagram Effect* for a long time. As a college freshman I experienced a dark night of the soul and was hospitalized with clinical depression. After emerging from depression with the aid of some good therapy, I eventually discovered the Enneagram and learned I could use this potent tool on my own to maintain emotional health and live a vibrant life.

For sixteen years I have counseled people using the time-honored Enneagram to help people learn how to take their health and happiness into their own hands and live with more balance and joy—really, to feel *well*. Over my years of practice, I have developed a unique way of working with the Enneagram that has greatly benefited my clients, and I have witnessed the transformations that take place in their lives when they come to know the Enneagram the way I see it: a map to emotional wellness. I am writing this book to capture my approach and to disseminate this system to a much wider audience than I can reach through workshops and client sessions.

You may be asking, what is the Enneagram?

The Enneagram is an ancient holistic system that identifies nine personality types among all of the people who walk the earth. The name is derived from the words *ennea,* meaning nine in Greek, and *gram* (gramma), which means written. The system is depicted by a nine-pointed symbol, written with a star-like figure within a circle. Each point of the symbol cor-relates to one of the nine universal personality types on the Enneagram.

We all share the traits of all nine Enneagram personality types, but there is always one type that best captures the essence of who we are as individuals. In fact, in all my years of doing this work I have never met a single person who, upon learning about the specific characteristics of their own personality type with me, concluded, "No, sorry, this isn't me." Instead, I consistently hear something along these lines: "Yep, this is me," or "Wow, this really is how I am," or "Oh, yes, this is what I do all the time!" or "This is incredibly accurate, and it's so helpful to learn this." One person even asked, "Wow! How do my Enneagram results know my inner map of reality?"

In my Enneagram-based life coaching and teaching, I have witnessed tremendous breakthroughs in my clients and students that practice emotional wellness, including the shedding of long-held patterns that have not served them well. For example, when a Type One, the Good Reformer, learns to let go more and accept that "It's not always my problem" as opposed to following their tendency to solve every problem or reform every person, a healing occurs. Or, when a Type Nine, the Peaceful Mediator, learns to practice conflict resolution instead of following their tendency to run from conflict, they forge a stronger connection to their authentic self. As they develop numerous insights into who they truly are at their core and why they have navigated their lives and their relationships as they have, they experience a kind of renewal.

Within this remembrance of who they are meant to be, my clients find new motivation to increase their emotional wellness. When they come to understand the nature of the nine personality types that coexist within all of us—and especially when they study their own primary type—the thoughts, beliefs, and behaviors they have typically engaged in, for the most part, unconsciously, suddenly come into sharp relief. It all makes perfect sense! Regularly returning to your Enneagram and specifically the wellness map within it, results in a new awareness that causes healthy shifts in behavior and empowers you to live a more resourceful and spirit-filled life. It is my hope that this book will contribute to the world becoming a more enlightened, unburdened place, one person at a time.

The following historical brief was one I received from Dr. Jerome Wagner, in my training. "It is not clear exactly how old the Enneagram system is, though there is evidence of it in texts dating back several centuries; for example, a variation of the Enneagram symbol appears on a 17th century textbook written by Jesuit mathematician Athanasius Kircher. Some believe its origins lie within the teachings of sacred geometry. The contention is that mathematical thinkers such as Plato and the neo Platonists might have arrived at some of the early Enneagram variations, which were based in part, on the nine celestial bodies in the sky. This is not certain, however, it is safe to say the Enneagram began somewhere between 2,500 and 4,000 years ago. It is also believed that there were variations of the symbol which merged into the one used today, namely a typology of nine personality types for those interested in psychological and emotional growth and spiritual connection.

Enneagram knowledge and variations have surfaced in each of the three mainstream faith traditions. *In Judaism*, it was taught originally through the philosopher Philo. It later appears in the Kabbalah as the Tree of Life, sometimes called the "Tree of Nine-Foldedness."

In Islamic traditions, the Enneagram symbol is believed to have been left to us by the Naqshbandi order of Sufism, also called the Brotherhood of the Bees, (collectors of knowledge). The Symbolists, who taught through symbols, may have created the actual Enneagram symbol in the fourteenth century.

In Christian traditions, the mystic Ramon Lull, who was influenced by his Islamic studies, may have been one of the first to pass it on to other Christian institutions. It may have been referred to as The Nine Points.

Another more recent (1970s) contributor to the Enneagram was Oscar Ichazo. He taught and expanded Gurdjieff's laws of the Universe (the nine points) to see these laws operating in the human being, thus providing some psychological clarity to the nine points. Claudio Naranjo, a Chilean psychologist, (1990s) learned the system from Oscar Ichazo. He also facilitated its introduction to Western culture, using psychological language to make it easier to understand."

Since the 1970s, the Enneagram has become increasingly mainstream in self-help and spiritual circles; indeed, many I have met are not affiliated with a traditional religion, though often spiritually inclined. On the other hand, some students have let me know that they are agnostic or atheist and are interested in learning about the Enneagram to better themselves.

People whom I have studied with include Jerome Wagner, Russ Hudson, the late Don Riso, Helen Palmer, and the late Dr. David Daniels, to name a few. They have all contributed greatly in their particular point of view, and here in this book, I contribute mine.

The Enneagram is a great relationship tool, especially for the foundational relationship with the self, and holds within it a powerful compass back to our authentic self, our essence. It is the quality of the relationship with the self from which all other relationships are formed. If we attract people into our lives who hold similar levels of function and dysfunction, then our self-growth work for awareness and wellness is a chance to raise the vibration for all concerned. With our own growth we can see a ripple effect in the lives of those close to us.

There is a lovely anonymous quote that you may have seen on a refrigerator or desk that says, "Peace, it does not mean to be in a place where there is no noise, trouble or hard work. It means to be in the midst of those things, and still be calm in your heart." We could substitute the words "security" or "centering" for peace and it would be just as profound.

Most of us, upon hearing this adage, think, "I'd like to know where I can get more of that!" Practicing the wisdom and the wellness map of your type on the Enneagram gets you more of *that*.

Glossary of Enneagram-Speak, A Quick Overview

Strengths and Challenges: resourceful and less resourceful states of being

Emotional Passion: our driving energy; like emotions, it is not right or wrong but is best when it is worked through and managed; contributes to what makes us "tick."

Area of Avoidance: our blind spot; falls under our shadow, which means either we are not aware of it or we deny it.

Wellness Map: shows us our specific wellness map; states of centering, and well-being or states of stress, un-ease and disconnection; shows which corresponding type's high side floods into your personality when you center, and which corresponding type's low side sneaks into your personality when you allow yourself to stress or be disconnected, Wellness Map shows us how to get back to center. Knowing your wellness map often resonates deep within and motivates you to live more often from your strengths.

Peaceful Mediator

Powerful Protector   8   9   1   Good Reformer

Joyful Adventurer   7   2   Loving Giver

Loyal Skeptic   6   3   Effective Achiever

5   4

Wise Observer   Original - Romantic

Wings: we have two wings and usually one of them is dominant; a preferred wing style influences our core personality type. The wings are the next door neighbors of your type.

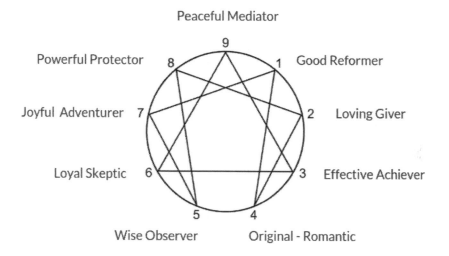

Instinctual Center: Is your preferred place to hear your instincts, your *knowing,* in your head, heart or gut center?

INTRODUCTION
TO THIS BOOK

T he first nine chapters in this book give an understanding of each of the nine universal Enneagram types. I begin each chapter with a short story of the type. I then cover the seven mainstays of each type. They are:

1. Strengths and Challenges of the type

2. Emotional Passion of the type

3. Area of Avoidance of the type

4. Wellness Map of the type

5. Instinctual Centers of the type

6. Wing Style of a type

7. Ways (for the type) to practice balance

The remainder of the book speaks to the Enneagram Effect, specifically its wisdom and practice, on your life, and what the trajectory for your life can look like when you practice thriving, not merely surviving; in other words, when you are acting in alignment with who you are meant to be.

If you are new to Enneagram inner work there is a personality type discernment quiz and a list of songs that I like for each of the Nine Types.

The Strengths and Challenges section for each type, while certainly not exhaustive, will hopefully give you a good feel for what each type can bring to the table of life.

The Emotional Passion section – or as Dr. David Daniels referred to it, the "driving energy" – is next. I like both terms because I think they help flesh out these underlying programs within us. I believe they are not right or wrong, but just are – it is how we direct them that will make the difference.

The Area of Avoidance falls under our shadow selves. This means that we are either unaware of it or we know of it and don't like it in ourselves. It is also called our "blind spot," and aptly so. For example, a Peaceful Type's area of avoidance is conflict. Resolving conflict is their task and their tendency is to run from it or avoid it altogether. In this section we'll learn about the area of avoidance for each of the Nine Types.

The Wellness Map for each type on the Enneagram is a term I developed and began using in my workshops. You may have heard it referred to as the arrows or the points of integration or disintegration. I call it simply a Wellness Map because it illustrates, in a very specific way for each person, what it looks like when we are in a state of balance and well-being. I actually refer to this high end of your type (which then attracts within you the high end of your corresponding type) your authentic and happy place; your "heaven on earth."

Conversely, we see what it looks like for us when we are stressed, in a state of unease, or in an absence of wellness. "House on fire" kind of stress can bring out the best in us, but the wellness map (arrows) shows us what we do to ourselves, where we go, and how we domino down when we choose to react from our "low side" to every day stresses. I call this state your "hell on earth." Of course to one degree or another we can go in and out of these states of center and stress all day long because we are human. Our ease and inner security can go hand in hand with our authenticity, and our dis-ease may be influenced by our repeated abandonment of our true self.

The Wellness Map shows us that when we choose to be in a place of inner safety and security, we are closer to our authentic self and more connected to our essence in Spirit. In the movie "Life is Beautiful," the father chose to make the best of an otherwise unbearable and stressful time in a concentration camp. He chose to make life beautiful for his young son by playing imaginary games, thereby shielding him as much as possible from the horror of the situation. He was extraordinary, and I love his example because it so beautifully shows us that we can choose to feel safe, secure, and beautiful, or not.

When we do this inner work, of choosing security over stress, we pull in or attract the many resourceful gifts within our unique personality. It is when our personality is driven by Spirit, where we are perfectly safe, that we find ourselves directed, joy-filled, enough, secure, resourceful, and so much more.

The Three Instinctual Centers, which are divided among the nine personality types are most easily remembered as the heart center, the head center and the gut center. You will learn which center your type favors and how it looks when it is on overdrive, as well as what can be achieved when all three are balanced. My hunch is you will recognize your instinctual center if you can be honest about your patterns in times of stress. Each of these centers holds untapped intelligence for us, and our goal here is to align all three for better self-mastery.

When the *heart-centered* person is on overdrive, it can look like drama outbursts. This is accompanied by the sense that your emotions are engulfing you instead of informing you. In some cases your feelings may have been neglected for a long time.

The Heart types include:

Type 2, Loving Giver

Type 3, Effective Achiever

Type 4, Original Romantic

The *head–centered* person, when stressed, gets into the monkey-mind, so called because your mind jumps around in your head the way a monkey jumps from tree to tree. Your mental wheels are spinning, but your problem-solving ability goes nowhere.

The Head types include:

Type 5, Wise Observer

Type 6, Loyal Skeptic

Type 7, Joyful Adventurer

If you're a *gut-oriented* person, you have a lot of "knee-jerk reactions," hence the word jerk. These reactions, in times of trouble or stress, often are not accurate, and feeling like a jerk, you wish you could take them back.

Gut types include:

Type 8, Powerful Protector

Type 9, Peaceful Mediator

Type 1, Good Reformer

The Wing styles are, as the name suggests, the core types' wings; the "next door neighbors" of the type. For example, Type Nine, the Peaceful Mediator, has Type Eight, Powerful Protector, and Type One, the Good Reformer, as its wings; one wing style will be dominant and will affect the core personality type. The various wing styles for each type are as follows:

Type 1: Good Reformer's wing style is Type 2 or Type 9.

Type 2: Loving Giver's wing style is Type 1 or Type 3.

Type 3: Effective Achiever's wing style is Type 2 or Type 4.

Type 4: Original Romantic's wing style is Type 3 or Type 5.

Type 5: Wise Observer's wing style is Type 4 or Type 6.

Type 6: Loyal Skeptic's wing style is Type 5 or Type 7.

Type 7: Joyful Adventurer's wing style is Type 6 or Type 8.

Type 8: Powerful Protector's wing style is Type 7 or Type 9.

Type 9: Peaceful Mediator's wing style is Type 8 or Type 1.

In the Ways to Practice Balance section, you'll see how you find your power when you are centered. When you live from your spiritual power, you lift up everyone around you. Each of the nine types brings an amazing abundance of gifts when balanced.

In conclusion, you will see how the Enneagram Effect can manifest in your life and you can begin this process by taking the discernment quiz at the end of the book.

Emotional Wellness and the Enneagram

In my Enneagram teaching and spiritual coaching, I've come across people who learned it in the 1970s, 1980s or 1990s. They found it fascinating as many people do, but they focused on the intellectual aspect of the Enneagram.

It is important to learn about the nine universal personality types, and your type in particular, for becoming more conscious within and about your personality can bring a certain grace or direction. However, it does not stop there.

My passion for teaching and coaching with the Enneagram is rooted in what was perhaps the most difficult time of my life, when I had to make a meaningful inner life a priority in order to get well.

I knew nothing about the Enneagram during this dark night of the soul, which I experienced intensely ("acute" was the clinical word) as a young adult. It was also a most powerful time in my life because it resulted in a reopening to my authentic self.

With awareness, over time, the tapestry of one's life can make so much sense. When I was in this darkness, I had no idea of the many wonderful openings that I would find along the way. I certainly didn't know that my hard work on my own individuation, as Jung called it, would be the foundation from which I would draw my inspiration to assist others in their own inner work.

My descent into the dark night experience begins on a beautiful mid-October morning my first year of college. I had been attending a local city college and deeply unhappy about it. Lost without my high school friends and siblings who had scattered off to different colleges and experiences, I'd been living at home, resisting the big scary world, and hating myself because of it. I had been doing my best to power through, choking down my fears with my tasteless and scarcely eaten breakfast each morning, then sliding into the passenger seat of my father's car. He would drop me off at school then continue on to a nearby Jesuit university, where he was a Communications professor.

I really wanted to be at that university, but he was a strict father and after watching my sisters clash with him over their studies and social life there I was afraid to go there. While in high school I had worked part time at a doctor's clinic, so exercising a snippet of independence, I made a decision to go to the local college for their nursing program.

I had been depressed because I wasn't doing well in the science courses. In fact, I had a hard time concentrating in any class, never mind "getting down" the coursework. Being more of a creative, communicative type, I had known the sciences would be challenging but the service aspect of a career in nursing appealed to me.

As I sat in class this particular morning I was feeling particularly shaky, anxious and weak, but tried to hang on. At the keyboard, I could not distract myself from these doubts anymore. As Kenny Loggins sings in his hit song, "This Is It," there was "no room to run, nowhere to hide." Fear and guilt loomed large and e v e r y l e t t e r on the keyboard represented something painful, that is, a doubt or fear I had about myself. My head hurt. I was losing the race against myself.

I put my head down in my arms and the counselor came in. She was gentle, kind and beautiful, like an angel, with a lovely, pulled together outfit and perfectly manicured nails.

We had a short talk about how confused and alone I felt, how unhappy I was, how I wanted to be at the university where my father taught and yet, I wanted to break away. I thought Nursing was a good career choice, but I have never excelled in any science class. She saw my deep exhaustion and kindly said, "Don't worry, it will all work out for the best. I have called your mother and father, and your father will be coming from work soon."

After what seemed like only minutes, my father was there, asking in his professorial and concerned voice, "What seems to be the problem?"

"I don't know who I am," I said through my tears.

He simply said, "You are a child of God."

Drowning in despair, I managed to get six words to the surface: "I don't know what that means."

My mother, a Midwest farmer's daughter, was a kind and peaceful type. She found conflict and tension difficult, and denial easier. She was a fervent believer in the power of prayer and often thought it alone could be the answer to everything.

My father, a loving if overbearing type, took charge and said, "By all means, prayer, yes, but something is deeply wrong; she has not been well for weeks, and we need to take her to a doctor."

When I met my therapist, his kind blue eyes seemed like a soothing ocean. "Are you feeling a little confused?" he asked with great kindness and compassion, and even now, I clearly remember feeling a good chunk of the house I'd been carrying on my back slip off and fall away.

"I feel like I'm going crazy," I told him, and was relieved when he replied that crazy people usually don't realize that they are crazy.

"No," he said, "You are just a little dependent and not liking yourself very much because of it."

I would learn that I lived in a world of too much black and white. A world in which parental over-coercion or force, mostly on the part of my father, eliminated a lot of my self-expression and development.

Ours was a large family – I was one of six children – and my parents ran a "tight ship." They were good people. I knew I was loved, but there was a tone in our home that was, during times of stress, equal parts love, and equal parts guilt and fear. The part of me that held irrational guilt, and fear and internalized anger, or, depression, was eclipsing the part of me that felt okay. This ambivalence would be a large and looming monster until I learned of its gifts to me; and depression would turn out to be a creative force in my development. Growth often feels like betrayal at first.

Gradually, I found my way back to myself. It was a long and powerful process, intensely painful for the first three months, with many challenges throughout the first year. There were some steps forward and some back until I graduated from college, but once this door to myself opened wide, my commitment to my emotional and spiritual health grew and, like Alice in Wonderland, opened door after wonderful door. I found a meaningful career, married the love of my life and raised a beautiful family. These things I know may not have happened if not for the dark night of my soul, and I often acknowledge it with a healing affirmation that my friend Dr. Darren Weissman created for his Lifeline work: "infinite love and gratitude."

My enlightenment through the Enneagram came in mid-life. It was a few years after our fourth child arrived and my mother passed away. After a culmination of these and other experiences, I experienced a deeper call to transformation. I left the corporate world and went back to school to get a Master of Arts in Pastoral Studies. On a windy day at the university lake campus, I asked God, "How can I do this sacred work of psychological and spiritual direction? I am just damaged goods like the rest of us…"

Immediately, I heard deep within me, "I will put the words inside your mouth." It was a moment of intense and very clear intuition.

I've been following that voice for sixteen years and taking it to whomever will have me, teaching in homes, in educational, holistic, civic centers, business and even cruise ships. The work has given me a deep and lasting joy.

I love to teach the Enneagram not only because it is widely accepted, but because it is received with such enthusiasm. If you look up the origins of the word *enthusiasm* you'll find its original meaning is "God in us" or "divinely inspired." This is evidenced by light in my students' eyes as they become more self-aware and compassionate, and through all I learn from them every time I teach it.

I believe most of us want to grow; we're just sometimes unsure of how to do the growing. Oftentimes our upbringing and religious traditions have failed to show us the most effective way to get there, and as the saying goes, old habits and patterns do die "hard."

For many people, it takes further internal work to sort out the spiritual forest from the religious trees that have gotten in our way. It is the bigger spiritual picture that most of us crave and want to reconnect with. This is what the Enneagram gives to us.

When I was growing up I thought to be holy was to be perfect. How freeing to learn through my own healing work, and later, through the Enneagram, that wholeness is a *process*. For me, this process is best experienced through a practice of "being truthful till it hurts" kind of self-awareness. Self-acceptance often follows, however, even after you have committed to awareness, it still takes courage to take an Enneagram profile and psychologically undress yourself.

I came to a crossroads of sorts while in graduate school. My professor, Dr. Jerome Wagner, was getting deeper into the Enneagram material, and as we explored the types, warts and all, I found myself experiencing anxiety and a critical perfectionism – my "go-to" places during times of tension and stress. It brought up an urgent question.

I asked, "If we have developed our personalities by the time we are four or five years of age, and our patterns seem ingrained, how do we break out of our box, be masters of our ship and live at the higher end of who we are meant to be?"

The class was very quiet, and, no doubt noting their anxiety, Dr. Wagner quipped, "Oh we do it about a minute a month."

His attempt at comic relief worked, as evidenced by the chuckles around the room. I, however, had experienced a powerful aha moment. I looked past the exaggeration in his statement to the essential truth of it. Surely with the right guidance people could be conscious for more than a minute a month. We could make choices with increasing self-awareness and work to grow our self-control and balance. When we could not, we could admit that we were "beside ourselves," or disconnected. Emotional wellness could be a priority. If we do not have awareness we don't have much chance of changing ourselves. The wisdom of the Enneagram never preaches perfection – just conscious process – and I decided I would become a missionary of its wisdom, its offering of higher consciousness.

Imagine a world with more awareness, where people (where leaders of countries!) are aware of their area of avoidance or what issues they were in denial around. Imagine the freedom of standing in our truth and not projecting our shadow aspects onto others. Or a world where people do not run on autopilot with their emotional passions, but are more aware of their programs such as correctional anger, pride, self-deception, envy, avarice/withholding, fear and doubt, distraction, control, and self-forgetting.

Imagine being committed to self-awareness about your particular automatic responses, in the same moment that emotional passion gets triggered. This includes leaning in to it, naming it, handling it, and finally managing it or directing it, and not the other way around. Imagine a world of people who are intentional about having good emotional health and who can see more clearly how it affects their physical health. Think about the consequences of a more conscious world for couples, friends, families, companies and even countries. The potential for our greatness within this inner work is staggering.

Stress is a reality, but this inner work is about making it less of a reality in our lives. There are many ways to let stress go, including exercise, meditation and good self-talk. In the real world, letting stress go is easier said than done, but the good news is the Enneagram gives us practical ways for gaining consciousness and making more resourceful choices that come from our centering ability, not our often self-generated stress. One effective way to become reconnected is to breathe into the very passion that gets triggered. More of the science on breath work and its effects will be explored later in this book.

Awareness is like anything else – we get better at it with practice. Our consciousness rises to new levels, and from this higher consciousness comes strength, clarity, and empowerment. This spills over into our immediate and larger community.

If you are reading this book, you are interested in your self-awareness and its effect on others in your life, so you may already know this simple but profound anecdote.

There was a student who asked his master, "What is the most important thing I can learn in life?" The master replied, "Awareness."

"I know, master," the student said, "but what else must I learn?" and the master replied, "Awareness."

Again, the student said, "I realize that awareness is good, but what, other than that, must we learn in life?" and the master replied, "Awareness. Awareness. AWARENESS."

CHAPTER ONE

Type One, The Good Reformer

"It is not always your problem to solve."

A Short Story of a Good Reformer

In my workshops I often tell a short story about Claire, our firstborn. She falls within the One on the Enneagram, also known as the Good Reformer Type.

I am remembering how even as a six-month-old baby, she would see and point at tiny little details. People often told me what a good baby she was, and there was no doubt in my mind that, like all of us, she had come into the world a certain way. This distinct way was confirmed by all those who mirrored her good behavior back to her.

Often I would respond to all those "she is such a good baby" comments by saying, "Oh she has her moments, believe me." I did not want a "perfect" child who would later have a perfectionism disorder. I didn't know anything about the Enneagram back then, but I knew about emotional health and balance, and I *wanted that* for her as well as for myself.

My parents told about a time they were caring for her when she was two and a half years old. My father opened the door to her room to find her sitting up in her crib.

"Hi Claire-bear," he said, "What are you doing?"

She was looking at a book in her careful way, certainly not yet a reader in the true sense, and said, with a touch of annoyance in her voice, "Grampa, can't you see I'm reading?"

In that question to him we can see her Good Reformer personality with her emotional passion of correctional anger, or irritation, already developing.

Said differently, she had, from the get-go, a penchant for detail and concentration and *a right way* for all that she saw. In my mind, she came in to this world wanting to see and study the perfection in all that she saw. Somewhere along the way she got wounded, as we all do, and reacted like the Good Reformer, Type One, that she is. As Dr. David Daniel's writes in *The Essential Enneagram*, "[Ones] came to believe that their good behavior was expected and their bad behavior and impulses are judged negatively and punished, so they learned to gain love by being "good."

Good Reformer types, as I say, then become people who just see a way to make things better.

I will say here because you cannot hear it enough, *there is nothing wrong or right with our emotional passion, or our driving energy, whichever personality type we fall into on the*

Enneagram. It is how we survive, and although thriving not just surviving is our goal, the Emotional Passion is our driving energy. It is what makes us tick. In the case of the Type One, The Good Reformer, that emotional passion is correctional anger. There is nothing wrong with correcting things or making things right or better, or even using anger to help you correct that which you must. Excellence is born of this very driving energy or passion, however, for our purposes of self-mastery and good emotional health, we need to drive the emotional passion. Said another way, we need to be aware of and manage our emotional passion and work it through, not have it drive us all around so that we spin our wheels and get "beside ourselves."

Fast forward to when Claire was a sixteen-year-old high school student. I was in my Master's program at the time and one night we went to the library together to do our work. I was exhausted from homemaking, mothering four kids, teaching part-time and graduate school.

I said to Claire, "It is getting late, time to go, I am exhausted …you cannot get blood out of a stone."

She looked at me and said, "Oh, yes you can. Come on, Mom, just write a few more pages for your paper."

This is another gift of the Good Reformer – painstaking effort!

These days, Claire uses her own Enneagram wisdom practice to let go of her critical self, as all Ones must do in order to experience their virtue of Serenity. She now has a daughter of her own, and I often admire how she uses her great disciplined ways to assist the baby's growth. One example of her conscientious centered parenting is to honor a baby's sleep schedule and not let her desire to run an errand or receive an invitation get in the way of that. Her consistency allows her baby to self-soothe in a way that is beautiful to see.

I hope you are getting a good feeling for the personality that falls within Type One, The Good Reformer.

The Strengths and Challenges of Type One, The Good Reformer

Strengths the Good Reformer brings to the table:

Hard work

Perseverance

Attention to Detail

Honesty

Dependability

Conscientiousness

Commitment to Excellence

Integrity

Justice

Kindness

Responsibility

High Ethics

Challenges The Good Reformer brings to the table:

Overly high expectations

Critical (of self and others)

Overruling

Uptight

Righteous

Perfectionistic

Rigid

Condescending

Judgmental

Relentless

Unrealistic

Easily annoyed, irritated

The Emotional Passion of Type One, the Good Reformer

"Follow your passion." We hear this so often it has almost become a cliché. While the intent of the statement (to live according to what makes our heart happy) is accurate, in learning about the Enneagram and the nine types of passions, it is in fact much better when you *direct* your passion. Following it, or being dragged all over town by it, often leads us down a painful path. This is why the emotional passion, or as Dr. David Daniels calls it, " our driving energy" has been given a bad rap. The emotional passion for each of the nine types on the Enneagram is associated with the Seven Deadly Sins, or Passions.

The truth is, there is nothing inherently good or bad, right or wrong with emotional passions, just as there is nothing inherently good or bad about emotions. It all depends on how we are utilizing them. When they are running us, these passions or energies can go on overdrive and land us in the muck. When managed and directed, however, they can be part of what makes us feel alive.

As someone who grew up Catholic, the word sin can be a button-pusher for me. Many of our elders told us we needed to feel bad for our mistaken behavior, or sins. I am not mad about that anymore. I know our parents and teachers meant well and were doing their best to bring up good kids.

How much healthier it would have been, though, if they had lost some of that punitive tone and said, "Sinning just means to miss the mark, and we all miss the mark sometimes." A game of darts would be a useful analogy. How much practice do we need to make the mark with our dart?

Self-mastery is like that, a process that requires practice. Every time you manage your driving energy or emotional passion and work it through, you are practicing self-mastery. Here, you are resourceful, connected, and happy. However, when the emotional passion runs you, you can be disconnected and/or out of control. You can say, "I am beside myself."

As mentioned in my anecdotes about Claire, if you are a Type One, Good Reformer, your emotional passion is *correctional anger.* You have a developed critical faculty, or said differently, your ability to be critical runs long and strong. You have high expectations. This means that you are just wired, natured, and nurtured to see how to make the world a better place. You bring to the table a sense of oneness and perfection in the integrity of it all. Ones know how connected we all are to the birds and trees, and Ones bring this gift of oneness to the rest of us.

When people don't seem to care or have the same integrity about things that you do, you want to correct them. It's not like you scream or are rude to them; in fact it's quite often the contrary. You can and often are kind about it but inside are angry. Or, it can be more like a sense of being "right," and that righteousness is a smokescreen for the correctional anger, or annoyance. As in "I'm not angry dear, I'm just right."

On the other hand, a Good Reformer having a healthy, balanced and connected moment will say, "This situation isn't right; I want to correct that person's behavior or this situation, but I have learned it isn't my problem to correct or reform it."

If the situation relates directly to the Good Reformer's own perceived "bad" behavior, then a healthy expression may be: "I am beating myself up for something I had no control of, and my expectations of myself here are completely unrealistic, so I am going to let it go." Taming your inner critic takes conscious work. Although you would rather connect to the whole by taking control of it and somehow correcting or bettering it, the truth is that you are making it better by separating from it and letting it go. This is the paradox and the task that Ones face.

When at age twenty-one, Claire was going through a tough time and being unfairly self-critical, I told her, "Claire you need to say to yourself, 'It isn't always my problem.'"

She responded with her typical honesty. "Oh, Mom, that's really hard for me."

"I know it is honey," I said gently, "but *that* is your work." Process – not – perfection.

The Area of Avoidance of Type One, the Good Reformer

The area of avoidance for Type One, The Good Reformer is anger. When people of this type tell me they don't feel angry that often, I reply, "That's because it is the area that gets avoided!" For some Ones, "angry" may feel like too strong a word. When I ask them about their tendency to get irritated or annoyed (rather than full-blown angry), they accept it.

Why do Ones seek to avoid anger? Well, if you grew up like many of us did, with parents and teachers who wanted you to be "good," *and* you had a predisposition or temperament that went hand in hand with being "good," and you found that moving toward being "good" got you the attention you needed, then you perceived your anger to be "bad."

Even if you didn't view it as bad per se, you might have learned it wasn't *necessary* to be angry. The thoughts about anger, as communicated by our caretakers, might have gone like this: "Good people aren't angry"; "Jesus was slow to anger"; or simply, "You should not get/be angry."

Anger, unfairly, got a bad rap, so you strayed away from it; or, you might have had a parent with their own rage issues, which scared you away from anger and made you repress it. Either way, the area of avoidance falls under your shadow, and that simply means you aren't aware of it, or you are aware of it but do not like it, and so you avoid or deny it. The truth sets you free and once you live from the truth you can actually see the gifts in the shadow, which develops to help you survive.

The emotionally healthy Type One, Good Reformer learns and owns that it is very okay to *get* angry and furthermore, *feel* your anger or irritation. Before you can let the irritation go, you have to hold it or feel it. Repressing it is not the way. As the late shadow teacher and author Debbie Ford taught, "If you name your shadow aspects 'Angry Annie' or 'Irritated Izzy,' you get familiar with these parts of yourself. When you are familiar, you are aware." If the irritation of the moment is masked in righteousness, you might name this aspect of yourself "Righteous Rita" or "Righteous Richard." Getting to know this part of your self is part of the truth that sets you free. If you fight it, it controls you.

A healthy question for Ones to ask themselves is, "Is it my problem to do anything about this? Or is it someone else's?" And when it comes to anger, remember: if you name it and claim it you can tame it.

Of course there are those times when the hot potato – the anger – will nourish your greater emotional health. The key is that it is more effective to feel the anger and let it go (or not) rather than denying it or covering it up with behavior you think you should have.

Here is a little story that illustrates how naming the area of avoidance (in this case, Type One's anger) can help you work it through.

One rainy day, two sisters were going shopping and got into a heated discussion about where to park the car. The sister in the passenger seat was a Good Reformer and as usual, thinking ahead.

"I think it's best to park here," she said, "It's closer to the restaurant where we will most likely go to after we shop."

The sister who was driving replied, "Well I think this is a good enough place right over here."

She made her case, then her sister in the passenger seat insisted her idea was better. A back and forth ensued, and the driver, noticing her sister's tension, pushed her buttons a little.

"You seem so upset," she said, "Why are you so angry?" to which the Good Reformer sister blurted out, "I'm not angry; I'm just right! This is clearly the better place to park!"

"Oh My Gosh, what did you have for breakfast?" the driver teased.

The tension might have escalated even further, but the Good Reformer had been working on identifying and working through her anger, instead of denying it.

After taking a moment to calm down, she said, "I am sorry; I didn't mean to say, 'I'm not angry, I'm just right.' I wish I had said, 'I'm not right; I'm just angry, irritated.' I thought it was better to park here. It doesn't really make a difference, does it? We are talking about a little walk – I'm sorry, you are the driver and can park wherever you want."

And just like that, the situation was diffused, all because the Good Reformer recognized her anger, owned it, and worked it through.

This might be a small example but remember, life is in the details.

Even if you aren't a Good Reformer, you still know what it feels like to be that sister in the passenger seat, and you can know the freedom of owning this aspect of yourself. An example of healthy self-talk is: "I was irritated or angry but I am not now, as I see it is not my problem to solve or reform."

This is a much more empowered place to live than the land of eternal "I/you should or should not…"

The Wellness Map of Type One, the Good Reformer

Within the entire nine types on the Enneagram there is a very helpful map that many of my clients like a lot and find practical to use. This is the Wellness Map, and it indicates which corresponding types a given personality type attracts within when either centered or stressed. In psychological terms these are "points of integration or disintegration," or more simply, "the arrows."

I call this the Wellness Map because to me wellness is the ultimate purpose of this growth tool. To this end, it assists you in deepening your self-awareness and compassion and helping you strengthen your connection to Spirit; it also gives you strategies for protecting that connection. This is the place within where you are most integrated to date, where you are safe, clear, inner- directed, joyful, et cetera. The wisdom of the Enneagram also takes into account the relationship between your emotional health and your physical health, and how this relationship plays out in in your behavior patterns, which stem from thoughts, feelings and reactions. The Wellness Map shows you very specifically what it looks like for you when you are in "a state" of security and safety, or in a state of stress or tension. Each personality type has two corresponding types that interact with it.

When the corresponding type's arrows are coming toward your type, you are receiving from the HIGH or resourceful side of that type. You are attracting within you the virtuous qualities of that corresponding type. You are being guided to your gifts and to your authentic self. It is when you feel the most complete, content; a kind of heaven on earth. It reminds me of that line in The Lion King, when Mufasa tells his son, Simba,

"Remember who you are." I think what he's really saying is, "Remember the *essence* of who you are." That is what the Wellness Map helps us with.

Conversely, when the arrows go away from your type, you are receiving from the LOW or less-resourceful side of the corresponding type. I like to think of it as a "domino-ing down" into the muck or gunk of your life. When the arrow in the Enneagram symbol goes away from your type, it literally means that you are going away from your authentic and essential self, to a kind of hell on earth. That is, you are abandoning who you are, and who you are meant to be.

The Wellness Map is a profound part of the Enneagram because it helps you realize that you can go in and out of making choices from safety or stress all day long. It is a natural tendency to react when in stress, rather than respond when centered.

When I was little, it seemed an insurmountable task to be good all day. What I did not realize back then is that when I make choices from my center, where I am safe and balanced, I make better choices than when I am in states of tension or stress.

When I come from "it is a process, and it is my choice," I naturally go to my center or well-being, my "heaven on earth," more often. I see a bigger and a healthfully detached picture, and from this perspective I realize that trying to be good or perfect is vastly different from being connected to my wholeness.

For a Type One, Good Reformer, the Wellness Map looks like this:

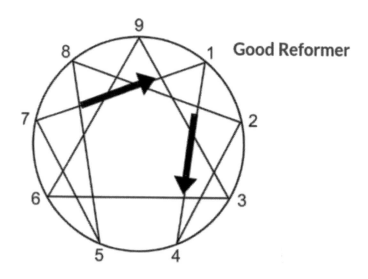

When you are centered within your own type, meaning when you are managing your emotional passion and are in touch with your area of avoidance, you unburden yourself and receive the enlightening aspects of Type Seven, The Joyful Adventurer.

When you hang on to your righteousness and rigidity as a One, you can domino down into more criticism of yourself; you may feel it from others as well. Then you get depressed and direct that anger toward yourself with a "Why can't I ever get it right like other people do? I am not special and feel so ordinary, less than ordinary" and so on. As you stress, you receive from the low or less resourceful side of the Original or Romantic, Type Four.

Let's return for a moment to the sisters in the car; how might it have gone if the sister in the passenger seat wasn't interested in stepping outside of her box, being aware and in acceptance of her challenges with anger and righteousness, and longing for the "ideal"?

Certainly, an unwillingness to look at your correctional mode can lead to more tension with others, an escalation in arguments (and/or fighting about other things) and quite possibly a miserable time for everyone involved. However when the passenger sister worked through her area of avoidance – her anger – she was able to manage her passion of needing to correct the situation or behavior of her sister behind the wheel.

Her Wellness Map unfolded before her as she chose to come from her center of security and safety and realize, without fear, that she was only human. She made the choice to work through the anger, thereby attracting the high end of Type Seven, The Joyful Adventurer, to herself, which in turn allowed her to unburden herself of the matter. Letting go of her sister's problem, where to park the car, gave her, as the passenger, a feeling of relief or lightening, and with it an overall sense of well-being. Life is in the details, and this seemingly trivial example illustrates the different outcomes we experience when acting from centeredness/security/safety rather than stress.

Deepening your awareness of your type and the two corresponding types that match your states of center or stress is a kind of inner work that reaps rewards. When you feel yourself on the downslide into the gunk/ LOW/less resourceful side, and can, in your new awareness, remember that Seinfeldian vernacular and say, "I am not going there," you turn on the inner GPS and course correct.

Is the transformation immediate? Will you, like the biblical character Saul, fall off your horse and have a complete conversion to a life of ease? Hardly. This is a process, but with practice of Dr. David Daniels' four As – awareness, acceptance, action, and adherence – we can transform into the individual we would like to be. With conscious practice, we can use our Wellness Map to go to the resourceful side of who we are meant to be. We see the trajectory for our life. It resonates deep within and this authentic aware place is our happy place.

The Instinctual Center of Type One, the Good Reformer

As mentioned in the Introduction, there are three instinctual centers among the nine universal types on the Enneagram. They are most easily remembered as the *heart* center, the *head* center and the *gut* center, and most of us favor one. Said differently, it is the "place" that you have the most "practice" in.

Type One, The Good Reformer is one of the gut-centered types. If you're a Good Reformer, this means that when disconnected or stressed and in reactive mode, your gut center might get over-activated, and along with it, your passion for righteous reactions and overly high expectations start running.

Someone else might point it out to you, and possibly, another reaction could ensue. For example, you might think, *What do they know?* You may even blurt out something you regret.

If you are in touch with this reaction and the origin of it, you may be able to easily catch it and apologize. Maybe not, and then you may have to deal with another outpouring of internal or external criticisms, or both. The important thing to remember is that you can do your best problem solving when you have aligned the three instinctual centers of head, heart and gut.

In order for the Good Reformer to connect and align the gut with the head center, he/she must learn to think things through before reacting. If you are on overdrive with reactivity from the gut center, ask your heart what it feels. Do you get a different answer? Ask your head what it thinks. Do you start to feel an alignment or agreement between the head and heart? Give yourself time to hear the answers to these questions. You just may find that the gut center is softening in agreement with the other two. This is the inner work of aligning the three centers. Slowing down the train helps. Breathe into your new wisdom. Know that deep breath work will support you.

In everyday tensions and stress, if you slow yourself down and align your heart, head and gut, your problems will be solved more easily. This alignment is also a way to access the essence of all nine types, since these three centers of head, heart and gut cover the nine universal types within each of us.

The Wing Style of Type One, The Good Reformer

The wings are the next-door neighbors of any given type on the Enneagram symbol. If you look at the Enneagram symbol below, you will see that on either side of each type's point there are two "wings," or arched lines. These lines make up the circle around the star. The Type One's wings, for example, are Type Nine, The Peaceful Mediator and Type Two, The Loving Giver, to the right. Remember, though you have two wings, according to Enneagram wisdom only one is dominant and influences the core type.

Peaceful Mediator

Powerful Protector   8   9   1   Good Reformer

Joyful Adventurer   7   2   Loving Giver

Loyal Skeptic   6   3   Effective Achiever

5   4

Wise Observer   Original - Romantic

In my sixteen years of giving Enneagram readings, I have encountered only a few people for whom both wings have equal significance to their personality.

This means if you are a Good Reformer with a Type 9, Peaceful Mediator wing style, you will have a different set of challenges/gifts in your personality than a Good Reformer with a Type 2, Loving Giver wing style.

If you are a Good Reformer, Type One with a Peaceful Mediator wing style, and if you identify with the high side of that wing, you may work through anger and conflict, and be conscious of managing your perfectionistic or overly critical tendencies. You may see grey areas rather than only in black and white.

You may note your tendency to blend in to a fault and then be the passive-aggressive victim later. You may see the value in asserting yourself and being heard directly. Your identification with the resourceful or high side of your Nine wing may help you feel strong compassion and forgiveness. Betterment is strived for but in a way that says *we are all in process.*

If, on the other hand, you're a Good Reformer who identifies with the low or less resourceful side of your Peaceful Mediator wing style, you may be critical and avoid conflict. This might squelch any chance to work through the anger or irritation you may be feeling.

Remember, the easiest way out is through the feelings. Pushing down our feelings over and over is like pushing down a beach ball under the water; they will just pop up in another place.

If as a Good Reformer you identify with the high side of the Loving Giver wing, then you'll manage your tendency to be critical or perfectionistic. You may also let go of the need for approval from others and speak up on your own behalf. You will want integrity and fairness, not righteousness, in your relationships.

If someone initially disappoints you because, for example, they do not give the way you give, you may see that this is not your work and let it go. You may meet your own needs, either by asking for someone's help or, as cliché as it sounds, being your own best friend and being very compassionate and generous to yourself.

An unhealthy response from a Good Reformer with a Loving Giver wing may be just the opposite. You may have unrealistic expectations of others and have angry, even vengeful feelings toward others or yourself.

Ways for Type One, The Good Reformer to Practice Balance

1. Learn to say and mean "It is not always my problem," and learn to differentiate which issues of betterment truly concern you. The world needs much improving, it is true, and one of the best ways for the Good Reformer to bring it about is to manage perfectionism and to work through the angers and irritations with the intention of letting them go.

2. Remember as a Good Reformer that you teach us about oneness and wholeness and that it is available for us all. Consider that in your letting go of reforming things, you are actually showing faith that all will be made well by forces other than yourself.

3. Bring your virtue of true serenity to the table. This is a way to better the world *and* your health. When you are irritated and not feeling content or peaceful, ask yourself if the issue is worth "getting your shorts in a knot" about. Oftentimes the answer will be, "No, not worth it – not worth my health, not my work, relationships, et cetera."

4. When you are stressed and tempted to be critical of yourself or others, ask, "Is it kind, is it necessary, is it true?"

   This is a discerning way to let go of a burden that was not yours in the first place.

5. Consider the human touch. Great music often has a human flaw, like when a voice gets throaty or even cracks a little. Think of how much more appealing listening to this kind of performance is than a technically

perfect but artificial "muzak" experience.

6. Intolerance for flaws can suffocate potential for creativity. Didn't it feel great when the teacher said "There are no mistakes in art?"

7. Practice "both/and" thinking instead of "either/or" thinking. Think shades of gray rather than too much black/white.

8. Did you know that in great Asian art, there is always a mistake purposely put into the piece? It serves as a reminder that we are always in process, and therein we are perfect. Practice this belief into your daily life, especially when your inner perfectionist threatens to take over.

CHAPTER TWO

Type Two, The Loving Giver

"Ask for what you need, and ask again because your best gifts come from a full well."

A Short Story of a Loving Giver

I know a Type Two, Loving Giver; she is nurturing, very creative woman, and though she is not artistic in the sense of painting or fashion design, she is generally very good with color, balance and room design. She used to come over when I was decorating a room and offer to give her input. She'd say teasingly, "Let's spend your money."

We often accomplished a lot together, and her assistance, whether it was arranging a few pieces of furniture or giving a room a completely new look, was really great. She also expressed a desire to redecorate her own home; however, I noticed that whenever I offered my help she found one reason or another to put it off. Finally, we made a plan to start on it. When I got there it seemed the areas she wanted to work on had been avoided for some time. When she finally got her living room done the way she wanted, I actually clapped my hands in celebration that she had made her own desires a priority.

As you probably have surmised, the house in the above story is symbolic of the self. The Type Two, Loving Giver's tendency will always be to take care of the other or, as implied in the above example, taking care of other's decorating instead of their own. They are very comfortable in a helping position and have to work on focusing on their own needs.

Loving Givers also have a tendency to remind others what they should be doing; for example, an older sibling who guilt trips a younger sibling by saying, "When are you going to visit Mom and Dad? You really need to go see them."

As the above example suggests, Type Twos often have boundary issues. They may not be aware of what their work is and what is not their work, business, or responsibility. When their own needs make them anxious, they may give in to the tendency to put those needs on the back burner and shift their focus on others. To the Two, it might seem that they are "helping" a family member. Their "big heart" (i.e. their mission to fix, save or rescue) can advance quickly into drama mode, especially when, for example, the adult siblings have a kind of pecking order. Of course, this can be a problem for those other siblings who want to make their own decisions.

The Type Two may then get easily disappointed, even mad, if you don't see it their way, saying or thinking things like, *No one cares like I do, goddammit!* This is of course not the healthy side of the Two, and such controlling behavior, no matter how good intentioned – can really set things off between the sibling or friends.

A healthy Two, on the other hand, may offer a suggestion but does not guilt trip another in order to assuage the irrational guilt or codependency within her own personality.

If her advice is not followed to her liking, she would say, "Oh well, not my work… not my business." Her inner work is to practice saying "this is not my work," and focus instead on her own needs.

Loving Givers may not even realize they are blurring the boundaries; to them it feels natural. Moreover, Loving Givers who are over-helping types may get intense in defense of their giving style. When I called a Two I know well on this, she replied, "Well, you don't know my heart." It was the perfect example of someone with this personality type using his/her "big heart" as a smokescreen for a boundary crossing. For these people, I suggest *equanimity* as a one-word mantra, for it reminds them that we are ultimately much happier when we are receiving as well as giving.

Author, Neale Donald Walsh says it like this:

…that love is not what you want, it is what you are.

It is very important to not get these two confused

If you think that love is what you want,

you will go searching for it all over the place.

If you think love is what you are, you will go sharing it

all over the place. The second approach

will cause you to find what the searching will never reveal.

Yet you cannot give love in order to get it.

Doing that is as much as saying you do not now have it.

And that statement will, of course, be your reality.

No, you must give love because you have it to give.

In this will you experience your own possession of it.

The Strengths and Challenges of Type Two, The Loving Giver

Strengths The Loving Giver, brings to the table.

Generosity

Supportive

Sensitivity

Good listener

Service-oriented

Interested in others

Personable

Empathetic

Attentive

Humble

Challenges The Loving Giver can bring to the table.

Guilt tripping

Plays the victim

Needy/Codependent

Smothering

Aggressive

Fixer

Busybody

Blaming

Manipulative

Represses own needs

The Emotional Passion of Type Two, The Loving Giver

The emotional passion or driving energy of The Loving Giver is pride. As mentioned before, just as emotions are not inherently right or wrong, emotional passions are not right or wrong, but rather like a program running on a computer.

When typing away on the keyboard, you are happy to have this program, as it assists and informs the task at hand. You know you have the ability to turn it off when you're not using it. It would be kind of strange if it was on too long or really weird if it *never* shut off. You are in control of the program. The same is true when you direct your emotional passion.

If you have great emotional health you manage your passion by getting very familiar with it. You may feel it rising within you and can feel how if you let it continue to run you like a program you will find yourself in a trouble spot. If you're a Loving Giver, you give to a fault, then get resentful when the person does not give back in the way you expect, or don't give back at all. Giving just to get – be it approval, accolades, or "pumped up" feelings – is a kind of false pride.

Pride is a program that runs deep within a Loving Giver, and the good news is you are not alone. We all have emotional passions that run deeply, whatever our personality type. Pride in yourself for offering help to another human being or creature who needs it is a wonderful thing. No man is an island. A Loving Giver teaches those around them how to get out of self-centered behavior and give to others. However, when your giving is out of balance with your own receiving, it eclipses your healthy equanimity and ultimately places The Loving Giver in a disconnected place.

When you manage the emotional passion of pride, you are practicing self-mastery. The question is, how can you use your emotional passion to your highest good? How can it serve you so you can have better relationships, knowing that the foundational relationship with the self is the one from which all others are drawn?

When you deepen self-awareness and self-acceptance and manage your emotional passion of pride, you give from a full well. You don't come from giving to a fault, then saying with bitter resentment, "No one loves like I do, goddammit." As you get more aware of this pattern within you, you may feel this resentment less and less.

What you are is God's gift to you; what you become is your gift to God. There is a co-creating from the start. It is within this co-creating and equanimity that the Loving Giver changes the mantra from "giving *is* receiving" to "giving *and* receiving." Changing one little word can help you manage your emotional passion of pride. It can also help you discern between true pride and false pride. How do you come from the pride that is true? By balancing your giving with your receiving; by meeting your own needs as well as the needs of the other. It is not always easy if your own needs make you a bit anxious, but getting familiar with them is a true and worthy goal nonetheless.

Balance is the key to well-being and spiritual power; it is primary ingredient to living a whole life. Great alchemists find the perfect balance. As a Loving Giver, you may feel proud of yourself when you volunteer to give the most time at your kid's school. If however you give and give and give without much attention to your own deep needs and self-care, you are standing on a slippery slope. Soon you may be giving from an empty well and will feel depleted of your resources. You may get resentful, and maybe even vengeful about this. You will need to find that balance of giving and receiving. You may also need to practice asking for help before you get mad and demand it, or label people as worthless non-givers!

The point here is that for the Two, the best giving comes when your own needs are also heard and met. Clichés, like "pay yourself first," and "be your own best friend" are true for us all, but especially the Two. Givers may err on the side of giving, as that is your tendency and your comfort zone, and because of this, your personal needs generally require better attending.

To start creating more balance in your life, ask yourself things like:

Am I giving so that I can feel needed and proud of myself? Am I making this very capable person dependent on me?" Or, in metaphorical terms, "Am I teaching this hungry person to fish or, I am getting all the fish for them, even though they could do it themselves?"; or, "Am I giving to a fault here and bringing stress with me wherever I go, complaining that I am stressed but secretly kind of proud about how much I am doing or giving?"

If you answered yes to these questions, good. This work is not about being perfect, it is about getting out of the patterns of your old box. It is about shedding old skins that no longer fit and it is about feeling great – more emotionally healthy and connected.

The next step is to practice meeting your own needs, rather than focusing on the needs of others. When your energy is more balanced, between yourself and others, you do not need to fix, rescue, smother, or blur boundaries. You practice knowing what is your work and what isn't.

Rest assured, the others in your life will feel the difference in you when you are giving from a full well, rather than coming from depletion, or obligation. This kind of equanimity breeds the kind of loving and true pride you ultimately seek.

The Area of Avoidance of Type Two, The Loving Giver

If you are a Type Two, The Loving Giver, your area of avoidance is your own needs. You tend to distract yourself with other people's issue's, problems, faults and so on, for you may find it easier than facing your own. The problem with this repressive approach is that it will eventually show up some-where, in your anger, aggression and even in your health.

Being unaware of this area or aspect in your personality can keep you in a box, that being your habitual patterns of thinking and behaving. It can keep you from growing emotionally and spiritually. If you have said, "Well that's just the way I am," when someone calls you on those patterns that is a good indicator that you are living in your box.

If you accept that you do have a tendency to avoid your own needs, and furthermore, can communicate this to others and claim your needs, your discomfort around self-care will begin to lessen.

Each time you practice "I am special too; I count here, too," you tame the tendency to avoid your needs. You will find yourself more readily and easily solving problems before you get too depleted and feel resentful for all you do!

Meeting or tending to your needs is always about solving a problem, be it a little or a large one. It means living with the discomfort and even anxiety at times that comes with paying attention to yourself.

A woman in one of my workshops said, "I know I give too much, am more comfortable doing that, than giving to myself. And I know I get angry or resentful or disappointed when others don't give the way I do, or do not seem to be as caring. The trouble is, I do not even know what I need at times, so it is just easier to ask others what I can do to help."

Similarly, a client of mine who fell within Type Two personality said "I don't even know what my needs are."

Uncovering and meeting her needs could be as simple as asking herself, "What food sounds delicious to me right now?" Or, "Would I rather treat myself to a manicure or a massage?" Little choices lead to bigger ones like, "Whom can I ask to help me with this project – I am going to get help, somehow." Another helpful self-reflection tool is the "fast pen method," in which you write the question "What do I need right now?" then answer it as quickly as you can. Insights will be uncovered.

Another way for Loving Givers to meet their needs is to tell themselves, "I often need others' approval and this time I'm enough, or what I have done, is enough." Meeting your needs in thought, feeling and action and making them a daily priority is a direct way to feel the love you crave. This is what Dr. Sue Morter refers to as the "Front-end not back-end model."

Practicing meeting your needs is good emotional self-care, from the kind of food you prefer, to expressing yourself and problem solving in your uniquely creative way. If you have good self-care in your beauty routine, but not in your emotional well-being, you need to tune in to this area more deeply. Baby steps help, and remember, your practice is part of the co-creating with the Universe. It will match your efforts, and within a short time you will see that self-care, even if it involves asking another for help, gets easier with practice.

We all like to feel appreciated. Seduction is what you must watch out for. Being seduced into helping out, or "butting in," is easy for a Loving Giver. It is important to tune in to what this seduction feels like. When you help someone who wants to be dependent on you or whom you would like to rescue, and you stop yourself before becoming entangled and drained, you are on the right track. You are getting clarity about how helping can be a smokescreen for avoiding your own needs.

Once the Two understands their area of avoidance it becomes easy to spot; their need to help can be traced back to a trouble spot in their own life. Their false pride tricks them into feeling good about doing something or giving something to someone, when what they really need to do is let it go, and say, "It is not my work; it is not my business." Or, as Dr. David Daniels suggests, "Use anger and rising distress as signals that you are not meeting your own needs."

As you may already understand from reading about the Loving Giver's emotional passion of Pride, you can see how false pride works hand in hand with avoiding your needs. On my teaching poster of the Enneagram, I like to circle the emotional passions in red and underline the areas of avoidance in green to remind us that when in a trouble spot, we need to STOP (reflect) at the emotional passion and GO (work) through the area of avoidance. STOPPING helps you recognize when you are being driven by pride and instead direct it or distill it so you are managing it.

GOING through the area of avoidance, for the Two, means working it through your personal needs, rather than avoiding them.

The Wellness Map of Type Two, The Loving Giver

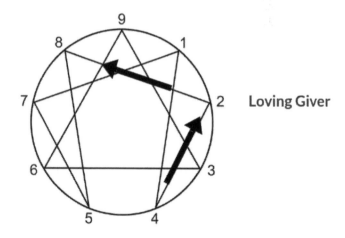

As mentioned earlier, The Wellness Map shows the corresponding type each core personality receives from or attracts within when he/she is centered or secure. It also shows which corresponding type they receive from when in a state of tension or stress or, said differently, when disconnected from self. Remember this map of wellness or a lack there of is indicated by the arrows on the Enneagram symbol. When the arrows are pointed from the corresponding type toward your core personality type, you are receiving the gifts from the high side of the corresponding type. You are moving toward your authentic self. When the arrows go away from your core type, you are receiving from the low side of that corresponding type. Think of this as going away from your authentic self.

Type Two, Loving Giver receives from or attracts within the high side of Type Four, The Original Romantic when centered or secure, and when stressed, his/her pattern is to receive from or attract within the low side of Type Eight, The Powerful Protector.

When receiving from the high side of Four, you may engage in healthy self-talk, such as, "I am a unique person, worthy of meeting my own needs, not just the needs of others." You are also conscious about your area of avoidance, or blind spot, and you work to stay awake to your needs, and accept them, not avoid them. In doing so you direct your pride to be the true kind of pride, not a false kind that comes from an overdrive to please and gain approval from others.

When you create this fairness and balance in your relationships, Enneagram wisdom says the Universe aligns with those choices. You may become committed to putting a dream of yours, however small or big, into action, rather than longing or wishing about your life. You have an idea or a creation and make it real. Lots of Twos are overtly creative, designers and such, while some tell me they do not feel so creative. I always tell them their creative bent doesn't necessarily mean they are painters or jewelry makers but are creative in their ideas or their quests. Your creative idea could be something as simple like, "I am going to tell my family what I need from them before I get mad at them for not reading my mind."

When the high side of Four pours into you, you may realize that making demands on others after they disappoint you is not as effective as asking them for what you need. When you say to yourself, "I am going to work at balance in my relationships," you'll see it helps you to stay in an assertive, not aggressive mode.

You might long for a cottage in the woods and set about to make that dream a reality. When you practice meeting your needs, not avoiding them, you receive original ideas and express them to others with creativity and presence. You find the sacred in ordinary things and give them more abundantly to yourself. When the giving and receiving are in balance, creativity and originality show up in your daily life.

This state of creativity and equanimity is what I like to call heaven on earth for the Loving Giver personality. Here you are integrating with the whole, and you are connected to your spirit.

When stressed, however, you are in a sense abandoning yourself to the low side of Type Eight, The Powerful Protector. Here, you want control. You can feel vengeful toward the people who do not love or give the way you do. You may become dominant, even bullying, and certainly aggressive, with an eye-for-an-eye attitude. You may decide you need no one, because they all disappoint. This is what I call your hell on earth.

When you domino down to the low side of Eight and find yourself in this aggressive or bullying mode, this is when you need to turn on the inner GPS and ask yourself, "Whose work am I doing?" Good questions to ponder are, "Am I avoiding myself to a fault here? Am I more comfortable talking of others than myself?"

The Enneagram and the Wellness Map within each type show you what it looks like for you when you are centered and safe, so that you can choose to be there more often. When you can get very familiar with your stressed out behavior, you can make a decision to "not go there," just one little victory at a time. You are adhering to your new behavior or practicing new ways. With a lot of practice, just like practicing piano or cooking or a new sport, you get better; it becomes your new healthier way.

All Loving Givers have ever wanted is to have everyone be free. Humility is your virtue.

Practicing your wellness map, giving up control on what concerns others, will allow you to experience this freedom.

To summarize, if you are a Type Two, The Loving Giver, your Wellness Map shows that when you are centered you are attracting within yourself the high side of Type Four (creativity and equanimity) and in times of tension and stress you are attracting within yourself the low side of Type Eight (co-dependence and resentment). Remember, though, that this is your general behavioral pattern. The Enneagram is a holistic paradigm. Even though we have a given personality type with patterns, and corresponding types, it is important to note that we can and do draw from all the types, both the high or low sides.

The Instinctual Center of Type Two, The Loving Giver

Remember, there are three instinctual centers – the heart, head and gut – one of which goes on overdrive when one is stressed. This is when your feelings begin to look like "drama."

According to Enneagram wisdom, if you are a Type Two, The Loving Giver, you favor your heart center. This means you often feel your feelings deeply and strongly, and can pick up on the feelings of others too. You are intuitive and are good in this place of the heart, because you have a lot of practice here.

When disconnected, non-resourceful or dysfunctional, you get overwhelmed by these emotions. Your heart goes from a trusted source and wellspring of inspiration to a source of drama. In these times you would be helped to balance your heart with what your head thinks, or what your gut is telling you. It is best to wait till all three centers are aligned, that is, giving you similar information, before solving a problem. This means when you are integrated or connected, and resourceful, you are informed by your emotional state but not dominated by it.

As you grow in your emotional well-being, you learn that your tendency to feel your way through things does not make you a slave to these feelings. In other words, you are not your feelings. They are a gift to you, serving you, informing you to your ultimate truth in the matter. You may feel overwhelmed with your feelings (heart center) but that is precisely the opportunity to balance or align these feelings with your thoughts, and knowing (head center) and bodily sensations, responses, (gut center.)

The Wing Style of Type Two, the Loving Giver

The Loving Giver has as its next-door neighbors Type One, The Good Reformer, and Type Three, The Effective Achiever. As mentioned earlier, usually one of these wings will be dominant.

If you fall within Type Two, The Loving Giver with a Good Reformer wing style and you identify with the high side of your One wing, you may claim and work through your anger when others disappoint you. You may refocus your love and compassion to own what is your inner work and discern what is another's. You will let other people's problems and work go more often. You may allow yourself to feel your emotions and then decidedly free yourself of the judgment or criticism and anger that you are feeling toward another, knowing it is often a projection of yourself. You will get back to the business at hand, namely, your own work and needs.

Anger can be productive in our problem solving, and the healthy Type Two with the One wing style will not push their anger away, but feel it to heal it and then work it through in a self-asserting, non-aggressive way.

If you identify with the low side of your One Wing, you may let the anger build even longer. We all get angry and critical and disappointed because we are human, but how long do you let the anger fester? Or do you hide behind a smokescreen of righteousness because you don't want to admit your anger? I had a friend who fell within a Type One, Good Reformer, who said, "I really never get angry." When I asked him "But how often do you like to be right?"

He said, "All the time."

If you are a Type Two with a Type Three, The Effective Achiever wing style and you identify with the high side of your Three wing, you may be a generous leader and team builder. A healthy, effective Loving Giver will know his feelings count and that they need to be worked through.

You will come from this philosophy: "What is ultimately effective is driven by my inner truth, not my outer role or image." Coming from my truth is an act of self-love. As I come from my own authenticity, I am meeting the deepest need I have and am being efficient and effective."

If you identify mainly with the low side of your Three wing an unhealthy response for you might be to go on overdrive with the giving or helping, getting caught in the "ought" and "should have" roles, ignoring your feelings and ending up resentful and depleted. It could also be manifested by focusing on performing and doing more projects in an attempt at avoiding your feelings.

The more a Loving Giver with an Effective Achiever wing style comes from inner truth and feelings rather than their outer image or role, the more they direct the emotional passion of pride. They will not have to reframe their failures as successes in disguise or run from mistakes and failure as often. Failure will be a part of life that as a human being is inevitable.

Ways for Type Two, The Loving Giver to Practice Balance

1. At your essence, you teach the rest of us how to give to others and not to be an island.

    Remember that your greatest potential may be to purify the way you give so that it has within it great balance.

Bringing that to the table may be your ultimate gift to show us your virtue of humility.

2. Your new mantra is now twofold; rather than just "Giving is receiving," it is "Giving is receiving and receiving is also a way to be loving and giving."

3. Understand that the best giving comes from a full well.

4. Find things and people that "gift or grace you" and cherish the feelings of gratitude within.

5. You have an independent and creative spirit; appreciating it may help you protect yourself from being seduced into fixing, helping, seeking approval from others, or being a one person rescue team.

6. Practice interdependence by asking for help regularly, and when people disappoint you tell yourself, "It is not my work to rescue or teach them." Then find a way to give to yourself.

   Expressing your needs to another is healthy, even if they do not respond immediately as you would have them do.

   Notice patterns of blaming others, emotional outbursts and even crying as a signal that you have been avoiding your own needs.

7. Use the "creative no" when you feel yourself getting depleted. "Let me think about" it is always a good answer. If they follow up, you, having had time to reflect on it, may have the courage to say "No, sorry, not at this time."

8. Recognize that rest and laziness are two different things; give yourself the gift of rest and good self-care. A lazy

day may be just what the Doctor within you ordered!

9. Remember, when your needs make you anxious and you'd prefer to help another, slow down the train and remind yourself to "pay yourself first."

CHAPTER THREE

Type Three,
The Effective Achiever

"To get to the door of your truth you must first pass through the door of your feelings."

A Short Story of an Effective Achiever

There is a paradox at work in each of the nine universal personality types. The paradox for the Effective Achiever is that you are doers and you prefer being active; however, you are more balanced when you listen to your strong inner truthful voice, which allows you to just *be*. In essence, the Effective Achiever illumines the truth that you are loved and worthy because of who you are, not just what you do. To the spiritually inclined person, the *who you are* is a part of the divine source. You do not have to do anything to prove that.

In this life we would not get very far without doing anything, and the Type Three, Effective Achiever learns early on that he/she is known in good part by what they do, not by who they are. The inner work of the Effective Achiever is to lead with their essence and authenticity, rather than their successful outer image, role or mask.

If you're like many Effective Achievers, the outer reality you've created does not always match your inner truth, or, said differently, your doing can get far away from your being. When your "doing" consistently trumps or outweighs your "being" in importance, how you are being or feeling can get forgotten about until you are depleted and everything comes to a screeching halt.

In this brief story we will look at the United States of America's personality type, which falls under the Effective Achiever. Father Richard Rohr taught us to discern the personality types of any given country. In the global community, the USA is seen as a leader. At the high side of our country's personality, Rohr points out that we show many of the strengths of the Effective Achiever.

As a friend of mine from Italy (and an admirer of the high side of America) is fond of saying, "When America gets a cold, the rest of the world gets pneumonia." This adage implies specifically that when we are ailing as leaders, others often feel those ills even more than we do.

He and I spoke about this at length. "When we recognize the value of all others," I said, "and when we operate in a global circle rather than a pyramid, then we are truly successful. When the United States participates in success this way, rather than constantly striving to be "the stand-out" player at the top, we are most effective. True leaders raise everyone up with their actions. When we take everyone with us on the high road, and continually learn from those at our side, we are successful."

I then continued, "When we do not manage our passion of self-deceit, that is, when we continually reframe things with a philosophy that we are here to succeed no matter what, even to the degree of eclipsing the views of other nations, we deceive ourselves about the real needs at hand, and we lose that leadership ability in the purest sense.

"When the United States makes image choices over feeling choices, we deceive ourselves into spinning our success-driven wheels, and come head to head with the very thing we like to avoid as Effective Achievers, which is failure.

"What kind of leaders are we at this low end? What happens when the USA goes on overdrive, continually reframing for success, even reframing themselves, with a winning personality, performing their starring role as chameleons for all in the globe? If we play this 'winning role,' avoiding failure at all costs without much regard for feelings or true needs in a given situation, do we not do ourselves a disservice?

"We have all been embarrassed by the 'ugly American' moniker, which is a personification of our arrogance and overdrive. And we have been proud of our true leadership ability at the highest level as well, when we have let true feelings and needs trump our need for approval and our need to stay on top. When our leaders set the tone of a true personal best, it will indeed take our needs and feelings into account."

The same is true of the individual Effective Achiever, whose inner work is balancing his/her being with doing. Being encompasses feeling. A healthy Three doesn't gloss over feelings but rather holds them before letting them go. You get a handle on what you are feeling and work it through.

Your interior landscape comes more from your inner truth, even if it slows down your efficiency.

With this practice you will see growth or success within your relationships. People can be as important as your projects. A healthy Effective Achiever does not make work more important than people or use the clever excuse, "actions speak louder than words," to rationalize over-action and lack of communication.

Whether an individual person, or a country, a healthy Effective Achiever is interested in inner truth, even if that lessens your popularity. You delegate and do not dominate the workload because of a drive toward success and a winning image, or an intolerance of any failures small or large. Our culture is permeated with an almost perpetual 24/7 mentality. As one friend said, "We are all running hard."

Arianna Huffington, in a May 2017 article in The Huffington Post, wrote, "We need to put time affluence (relaxation) on the to-do list." She continued, "How about redefining success to include a third metric, beyond money and power – time affluence, which will lead, without doubt, to greater well-being and deeper wisdom. Not a bad thing to put on top of our to-do lists."

As a Type Three, you can have difficulty relaxing, or you can look for approval, as that in and of itself is often mistaken as a success. When you are too focused on receiving admiration, your leadership and effectiveness can suffer, as the true needs at hand do not get uncovered.

When your roles define you and the masks that you wear within those roles eclipse your authenticity, and when, slowing down to sort out the feelings involved is last on the list, you fail.

"The truth will set you free" is a wonderful mantra for the Effective Achiever. The real truth about the Effective Achiever territory is this: deep down, you want your real truth, which is informed by your feelings and needs. It alone leads us to our inner law and faithful higher self. True successes come from this place of authenticity, not from becoming an expert chameleon or performer.

This inner truth stems from what Dr. David Daniels calls the Effective Achiever fundamental principle, which is that "Everything works and gets done naturally, according to universal laws."

The Strengths and Challenges for Type Three, The Effective Achiever

Strengths The Effective Achiever brings to the table:

Marketing/sales-oriented

High energy

Motivating

Active not passive

Vivacious

Positive

Leader

Likeable

Multitasker

Ambitious, determined

Challenges The Effective Achiever brings to the table:

Ignores feelings

Over-identification with roles

Ignores others feelings

Work-driven

Over committed

Opportunistic

Unwilling to delegate

Unwilling to listen

On overdrive

Shrewd, scheming

The Emotional Passion of Type Three, The Effective Achiever

The Effective Achiever's emotional passion or driving energy is self-deceit. That means if you are a Type Three, Effective Achiever or have an Effective Achiever wing style, you have a tendency towards self-deception based on reframing for "the win" rather than on your inner truth. Remember, as the Enneagram is a holistic paradigm, you may be familiar with this driving energy or passion of self-deceit even if you have a different core personality type with different wing styles.

Those who engage in self-deception tend to play a role. Their goal is success for the purpose of gaining admiration from others, even if that means not listening to their inner truth, even if it means their image becomes more important than their feelings. Managing the emotional passion of self-deception means slowing the "image" train down and ramping up the inner world of connecting to and working through feelings.

Keeping in mind that emotional passions are not inherently right or wrong, how does it look when this program of self-deception and reframing things for a successful outcome at all costs is running or managing the Effective Achiever, instead of the other way around?

Remember, The Effective Achiever is a doer and success-driven. At the very low end there is a drive to avoid any failures or mistakes, a drive for success at all costs, and an end-justifies-the-means mentality.

If you're a healthy Emotional Achiever operating at the high end you are aware of your passion and how much hold it has on you. You can manage it more often, and while your role in your work, for example, is important to you, you do not let it replace your feelings. You work through your feelings, and it might look like this: "Oh even though it might look bad to my boss to leave early Friday, I am depleted and exhausted and have given many hours beyond the call, so I am going to honor my feelings and go. The world and this company will do fine without me this time."

How do you get to this place? With practice, practice,

practice. Breath work during times of stress will help you identify your self-deception and manage it. Be in a pregnant mother's shoes for a moment; think of it like getting a handle on the intense pain of a contraction as you prepare for childbirth; with each deep breath you lean into your inner truth, which in turn helps you become familiar with your survival patterns. This is a life-long work and with this practice of being aware and accepting your driving passion, you will be better able to work it through and let go of it more and more.

Every time you consciously breathe into what you are feeling and work it through instead of denying it because of the "importance" of the so-called success of the situation, you practice self-mastery. When you value and listen to your own feelings you ultimately get better at hearing the feelings of others. When you consistently practice paying attention to feelings, you hear and come from your truth. You cannot get to the doorway of your truth without first getting through the doorway of your feelings.

When you are aware of and managing your emotional passion of self-deception, you become a neon sign that says, "To Thine Own Self Be True." You are loyal to your inner truth and have a commitment to your authentic self.

The Area of Avoidance for Type Three, The Effective Achiever

The area of avoidance for the Effective Achiever is failure. A little failure could be identified as a "simple" mistake. A big failure looks like a huge mistake, and could have big rami-fications. If you are a visual person, think of these failures ranging from pale aqua to intense turquoise.

Remember, one way your self-deception manifests is when admiration from others becomes the idol or objective. Then you will take on whatever role you need to play or put on any mask you need to wear in order to ensure a win. Underlying all of this is the avoidance of failure.

Again, there is nothing right or wrong about having goals and desiring success. Threes are the ones who teach the rest of us to "walk the walk" and not just "talk the talk." However, coming from a "winning at all costs" mentality is some of the stuff behind high blood pressure and "winding up for a war," to name a few ills.

At the low end, an Effective Achiever is living in a box, so to speak, meaning he/she over-concentrates on reframing for the "win." As he/she does not like mistakes or failures they may not be willing to delegate tasks and instead do the bulk of the work themselves in order to ensure its success. At this point, their self-deception is managing them.

Ironically, if you avoid failure to an extreme you may find yourself staring failure in the face. This can come at any point, including and perhaps most painfully at the end of life, when you might see your refusal to listen to your higher self as a personal failure. However, repeatedly choosing the path of *working through feelings* and *claiming your authenticity*, not the paths of *masks* and *roles,* will assist you in living as your best possible self.

The Wellness Map of Type Three, The Effective Achiever

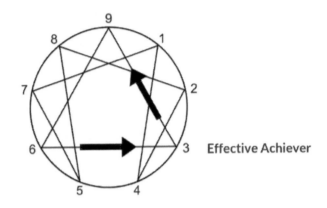

Effective Achiever

When the Type Three, The Effective Achiever is centered, Enneagram wisdom says you receive gifts from Type Six, The Loyal Skeptic.

When the Effective Achiever is receiving from the high side of Six, you can stop or slow down the proverbial speeding train of activity. This is when you say, "I need to stay with my feeling choice here, not a choice based on what others approve of or think is best for me."

Other examples of healthy self-talk include, "I was praised too much for my hard work, my ambition and successes growing up, but nobody really asked me enough what I was feeling. Well, it is time I do that for myself; what do I feel about this problem or dilemma? What is my real feeling about this?" Don't get discouraged if you do not have an answer to that question right away, especially if you are not well practiced in unpacking what you are feeling.

Another effective way to find out what you are feeling is to start with your area of avoidance. You might ask yourself,

"What failure or mistake am I trying to avoid here?" Remember to consider any failure, disappointment or loss, large or small.

The Wellness Map of the Enneagram has within it the law of attraction. The law of attraction says that when you put your attention on something, you attract more of it. This is true for the high and the low side of the corresponding types you attract to your type's specific map.

The Wellness Map of your personality type says that in stress, when you in effect abandon your higher self or essence, you attract more low energy or domino down. For The Effective Achiever, this looks like speeding up in activity and ignoring your feelings even more, or perhaps making projects more important than the people you interact with day to day.

You may end up so depleted that you numb yourself out through the computer, cell phone, or television, food or drink or whatever else is a narcotic for you.

The first step to changing this is awareness. Once you become aware of what you are doing in your less resourceful, or lower state, you can choose to let your inner GPS make a course correction. As you move back to the place of inner truth, you may feel a shift in your behavior that feels lighter. You will feel energized, and so will any teams you lead.

Charles Filmore, Co-Founder of Unity Church, speaks of deepened awareness (resourceful living) this way: "When we withdraw our attention, interest and support from the false and the unworthy, this is true fasting. When we give that same attention, interest and support to the enduring good, we are feasting on the things of the Spirit and this is true prayer."

In other words, true wellness is when personality connects

to spirit, and more than that, it is led by spirit. The Wellness Map shows you specifically what it can look like for you when you are choosing the state of security over stress. If you are spiritually inclined or not, choosing to feel centered, you consciously withdraw your attention, interest and support from the falseness Filmore describes. When you do this you are choosing to go to the high side of who you are meant to be, one who is connected to your essence. You also have more gifts to share with others. This is a process known as grace, and it is available to all of us all of the time.

As my friend and author of "Writing Down Your Soul" Janet Conner says, "Intention and attention (awareness within) equal less tension."

With self-awareness, you can see what happens when this passion or driving energy is running you with wheels spinning. You can see what your blind spot or area of avoidance is and work it through in problem-solving.

With each chosen moment, you can get a handle on the emotional passion and direct it. Initially when you let go of "automatic behaviors," it can feel strange, as if you are going against the grain, but you are going against only the grain of habitual reactions, because you are more than your habits. You are naming, working through and most importantly setting healthy boundaries for your passion, which leads you to your essential truth. You are working within the trajectory for your life that resonates and it will feel good to get out of the old, false way.

Each time you choose to feel safety and security over the stress, and feel your inner observer, you receive more grace. You are co-creating and the Universe will match your conscious efforts!

When this is happening, Enneagram wisdom and my experience agree that you will have begun activating your own Wellness Map. You have centered yourself and now receive from the high side of your corresponding type, where more gifts strengthen your core. When you do the work of this, and it is conscious work, it always feels good. Process not perfection, but in the process, you feel your progress!

For the Effective Achiever, when you work through your feelings and understand your many life roles as simply that – roles, rather than the deeper you – you will activate that inner knowing and receive from the resourceful Type Six, the Loyal Skeptic. You are developing a strong faith in yourself and, in the Universe, that all will be made well as you co-create with your Source.

When facing a problem, Effective Achievers can get some clarity by asking themselves, "What part of this problem is about my avoiding mistakes or failure? What kind of mask or game face am I putting on?"

Your healthy self-reflection may continue with these questions:

Can I resist my tendency to avoid failure at all costs and go on overdrive to make sure all gets done successfully?

Can I delegate or slow myself down and place some well thought-out energy to connect to a person on the team more than the project?

Can I stop and examine whether my emotional passion of self-deceit is running me all over town on a leash?

Am I reframing things and seeing them only through the successful lens?

What if mistakes were made, could I tolerate humiliation?

What if I make a feeling choice instead of an image or role choice, will the outcome ultimately be better because it was coming from an authentic me instead of a masked me?

This is the centering work, whereby your inner GPS course corrects and opens you up to receiving from the high side of Six. This is a good glimpse into the heaven on earth for the Effective Achiever.

In summary, your Wellness Map as a Three, The Effective Achiever is as follows: In times of centering and safety, you are attracting within the high side of Type, Six, The Loyal Skeptic (courage and faith), and in times of tension and stress you are attracting within the low side of Type Nine, The Peaceful Mediator (self-forgetting and avoidance of conflict).

This is your general behavioral pattern. Remember, though, that you *can* access the high side or low side of all the nine types on the Enneagram.

The Instinctual Center of Type Three, The Effective Achiever

If you are an Effective Achiever, you favor your heart center over your head or your gut centers. Right now you may be wondering how you can favor your heart center when you have a tendency to avoid your feelings and focus on role image or performance. It is precisely *because* you are heart-centered that when in stress your feelings seem overwhelming and you distract yourself with performance. Remember, the instinctual center can be thought of like as the information center or place within you that you are most practiced in to receive inner guidance. You can tell which instinctual center you favor, generally, because of where you go when in a trouble spot. I always ask my clients and students this question, and most know the answer immediately.

When the Effective Achiever is centered/connected and safe, you are tuned in to your feelings, but when you are stressed or disconnected, your feelings get amplified or out of balance. You may act it out overtly and yell, or more likely, you may unconsciously avoid tuning into your anger and identify with your role more than with what you're feeling. Stressed Effective Achievers get into overdoing and performing as a way of not having to deal with those feelings.

In order to balance the three centers, you need to quiet the drama of your heart and check in with your head and gut. To feel more centered and connected means slowing down and listening to all three centers to see if they are all telling you the same things about the problem at hand.

If your drama is still raging, that means you are out of balance and coming from your less resourceful side. In that case it is best to wait to solve the problem until you think it through *and* feel the instruction from your gut.

Where do you go when you are in a trouble spot in your life? What does your energy look like? Is it in your head, where your monkey mind takes over with too much thinking, analysis, obsession and restlessness? Or, is it in your heart? Are the feelings so big that you lose yourself in the overdoing, the role, image or performance so you don't have to feel them? If so, then the mask you are wearing is wearing you!

Helen Palmer puts it this way in *The Pocket Enneagram:* "Notice when activity is mechanical. Robot-like work suspends feelings." You know this place well if you are an Effective Achiever.

In order to be one step closer to your authentic self, you only need to pause enough to *feel* what is happening to you instead of moving farther away from your inner truth. "Slow down" is a great mantra for an Effective Achiever. Ten ways for you to slow down the train are in the Ways to Practice Balance section at the end of this chapter.

The Wing Style of Type Three, the Effective Achiever

Type Three, The Effective Achiever's wings are Type Two, The Loving Giver and Type Four, the Original Romantic, as they are the Three's next-door neighbors on the Enneagram symbol. Remember, one of these will be dominant to your core personality.

How might the wing styles influence The Effective Achiever?

An Effective Achiever who identifies with the resourceful aspects of the Loving Giver wing style will be more interested in equanimity in relationships. You will give more often from a full well, practicing good self-care instead of fixing or rescuing others.

You will be in touch with your feelings and with your team's feelings and make your feelings heard, both to yourself and to others. You will understand that no amount of obligation is worth burying your feelings. I think this is what St. Paul meant in 1 Corinthians 13: "If I speak human or angelic tongues but do not have love, I am a noisy gong or a clanging cymbal." If we do things out of duty, rather than out of love and authenticity, it means nothing.

If you identify with the less resourceful or low side of your Type Two, Loving Giver wing, you may be more influenced to give and do and do and give. You may let this overdoing or giving cover up your own needs and feelings, which in turn will ultimately build up anger and resentment.

If as an Effective Achiever you identify with the resourceful or high side of your type Four Original wing, you may be more sensitive and be able to share your feelings more often. You may understand that you must first accept or name a feeling in order to work it through or manage it. You know that feelings are not right or wrong, but just *are*. You may be more interested in being in tune with your deeper self and the depth of others.

Identifying with the high side of your Original Romantic wing style may help you relate or practice living within your own unique style, and this individualism may show up in your achievements. You may require something effective *and* original, meaning it has to have your own stamp on it or, even better, your team's stamp.

If you identify with the less resourceful or low side of your Four, you may keep your dreams on hold, spending too much time dreaming and longing and not believing enough in yourself. Your feelings might get all pent up inside because you can get too easily overwhelmed. You may squelch your dreams and say to yourself, "What's the use in trying?"

Ways for Type Three, the Effective Achiever to Practice Balance

1. Understand that your virtues of truth and authenticity are about the truth of your being, your Source, and not ego-driven over-doing. You are always a part of your Source.

2. Understand that love comes from who you are, not only from what you do.

3. Slow your pace down. Better yet, *stop*. Understand that a constant and intense pace puts up walls that do not allow you to truly hear yourself.

4. Dig deep emotionally. Be willing to face and feel your feelings, pleasant and unpleasant. Doing emotional work is easier with practice. Think of how practice contributes to success; use this concept to give yourself practice naming and claiming the emotion. Is it mad, sad, glad, or scared? Tension may be first felt as a sensation in your body. Use your words to identify it, for example, "I feel like there is a house on my back."

5. Practice asking yourself, "What is it I truly feel?" and listen carefully to the answer. Remember, a feeling will inform you and help you solve problems when you work it through. In order to let go of a feeling you need to hold onto it first.

6. Make feeling choices over image choices. For example you may say, "I *feel* guilty when I don't see my kids enough because of my work, but my role or image dictates that I should work late like all the other executives." Healthy Effective Achievers understand and own this feeling and realize that their projects need not

be substitutes for their relationships.

7. When you are in a trouble spot, start by naming your area of avoidance, which is failure, and work through your fears about it. Remember, leaning in to it and getting familiar with how you react to failures will help you avoid them less. With practice, failure avoidance will no longer be a blind spot for you.

8. You bring determination, motivation, and hard work to the table and you teach others how to get the job done and how to be an effective problem solver. Use this skill set to thoroughly face and stick with your personal issues as well.

9. Symbols are powerful when we are making changes within ourselves. Have something on your desk (i.e. a turtle) as a commitment to your new slower pace.

10. Write on a white mask in bold letters, and hang as artwork:

MY FEELINGS AND INNER TRUTH ARE MORE IMPORTANT THAN ANY MASK I MAY WEAR.

CHAPTER FOUR

Type Four, The Original Romantic

"Find the sacred in the ordinary and bring it to the world."

A Short Story of an Original Romantic

There is a story of a family who lost their beloved dog to an illness. While everyone in the family loved the dog in his or her own way, the primary responsibility for the dog's care fell to the mother. She was the one who took him to vet appointments and saw to his daily needs. In his old age she along with her husband got up to let him out as he cried in the middle of the night. Sometimes the kids would pat his head or pay him a small amount of attention, then run out with their friends. The mother knew that this was normal behavior for teenagers. She didn't expect everyone to stay home because the dog was sick, but she wanted to see that they *felt* as deeply about it as she did.

The illness went on for some time, and finally the family came to consensus that it was time to let their animal companion go. After that traumatic trip to the vet, the mother, who was an Original-Romantic type on the Enneagram, grieved in a deep way and felt the pain acutely.

She took up a lot of space with her pain and was dumbfounded and hurt that no one seemed to be as sad as she was.

The father replied in his stoic manner, "I'm over it, it's just life, it was his time to go." The kids all cried the first night and then they too seemed to be over it. This mother, however, could not get over it; she cried and moped around, saying how sad it was, how sad she was. When the family talked about the dog she would burst into tears and everyone felt sorry for her for they knew how much she loved the dog and how close she was to him.

The mother's grief started to feel so different in comparison to the others that she made an appointment to see a therapist. She wondered if something were wrong with her, as her feelings were often so "different" than everyone else. Her concerns were not entirely about the grief and loss of the dog, but in other areas of her life too. She just felt different and was feeling left out because of it.

She was tired of feeling disconnected in life, even from those closest to her. Was there something wrong with that? She wanted to know the truth.

The therapist explained that when it came to grieving,

whether it is a dog or a person or some other loss, everyone does it differently. It was very possible that the others in her family were still grieving, but in their own way. As for her husband, he might not have been in touch with his grief, or he might have been trying to appear strong for the others.

The teens might have cried or showed sadness in their way, whether alone or with their friends, but perhaps had mixed feelings about doing that with a parent. All of her family members might have also not wanted to burden her with their feelings because they knew how much pain she was in.

The therapist continued, "You are sensitive and feel deeply, but sometimes when those feelings come out, like water flooding a room, more water (emotions) from those around you doesn't feel like a good response from them. In fact, they can feel overwhelmed by all of those feelings, especially if they are fixer types, not feelers. And, in feeling overwhelmed, they may need to "dry up the water" and thus appear cold, or withholding, or overly efficient.

"You do feel deeply and your feelings are real to you, but you need to manage those feelings, not overwhelm yourself or others with the depth of them. Sometimes unmanaged feelings look and feel like drama, and this may be when others seem indifferent to you. Your feelings are very important but when they are so big and start to take over or eclipse how others are coping, it is time to reel your feelings in."

"But how do I do that?" the mother asked, "I thought it was good to feel deeply."

The therapist replied, "By breathing, exercising, talking feelings and thoughts out with a trusted, objective person who is not going to be overwhelmed by them. The object here is to work through, directing those thoughts and feelings so that you learn from them. You do not have to hold onto all the feelings that you have all at once or for too long a time. Emotions are fleeting, like clouds on a windy day. Noting and feeling your feelings is healthy but courting them for too long a time is not.

"You do need to hold them, that is, acknowledge the feelings and know that they are informing you of something. If the emotions feel overwhelming, all very intense and not easy to direct, that is when strategies like exercise, talking them through or writing them down, can help."

Ultimately healthy Type Four, Original Romantics know they are special and have a unique and equally worthy view. They know too that we all learn from each other and that the human race is not *in a race,* but made up of individuals with unique ways of self-expression. This includes how they grieve.

"You will come to see that healthy people who are grieving can express feelings in a range of ways, from crying and writing them down to dancing and exercising," the therapist added.

One woman I know who was in deep grief dealt with it by going swimming each morning. She couldn't talk about her loss, but as she moved through the water she felt stronger, like she was managing her sad and watery feelings. She shared that she *always* emerged from the water feeling better. As the therapist stated in the first story, each person has his or her own special way of grieving, and this woman did so in a very physical way.

We are all in this circle together. No one removes you from that circle but yourself. In having compassion for others and the way they grieve, you bring yourself back into the circle of love and life.

The Strengths and Challenges for Type Four, The Original Romantic

Strengths that the Original Romantic brings to the table:

Tuned in

Dreamer

Empathetic

Intuitive, psychic

Deeply feeling

Creative, aesthetic

Unique

Compassionate

Connected (to the whole)

Supportive

Personable, relational

Sensitive

Present

Challenges that The Original Romantic brings to the table:

Controlling

Abandoned

Disconnected from whole

Nobody "gets" me

Victim, long suffering

Misery loves company

Dark poet

Wild child

Drama queen or king

Feels ordinary

Excessive "if only" thinking

Melancholy

Rescuer

The Emotional Passion of Type Four, The Original Romantic

The emotional passion of the Original Romantic can be a one or two-fold experience of longing and/or envy. It is how you direct or manage the passion that makes the difference.

When can good come from an emotional passion? Longing for something and dreaming about it or even envying it can be the seed of making it happen. Think of baby steps. For example, I had a dream/goal of writing this book. The dream led me to go to the library three times a week to write without distractions.

On the other hand, being a slave to emotional passions, in this case, envy, would have meant denying my process of personal growth and self-mastery. Envying the authors who seem to crank out their works and beating myself up because I didn't work as fast would not have been healthy, or productive.

In these moments, an affirmation for you to say and believe is, "I have everything I need in this moment to grow, even if it doesn't feel like it... even if it is raining and grey for days on end and rain makes me tired, sleepy or sad, even if others seem to have it better than me. Be gone, envy, longing, and comparison!"

In her book, *"Gift of the Years,"* Catholic nun, Joan Chittester describes being under the spell of longing and envy: "Longing and envy has led us astray far too many times. What we wanted, we discover when we finally get it, doesn't really change much at all. We are still who we always were, restless and without direction. It is the present we really want. We want it full or empty, bursting or peaceful, but we want it. We concern ourselves too much with the past or future when we are not paying attention to the gifts in the present moment."

I remember being on the tennis court, playing in a team doubles match. I was over-anticipating our opponent's next move and feeling bad about my last careless shot. Those thoughts took away my focus. I said a simple prayer: "Help me be present to each ball that comes to our court and to each ball that we send to theirs." Yes, I pray through all of my tennis matches!

You may have heard the quote, *"Want what you have."* This is an excellent mantra, especially if you are a Type Four. When you do want what you have, you are practicing present moment stuff. You are content with and grateful for what you have right now. Remember, "Where attention goes, energy flows," and I would add, *it grows*! By *being* more of what it is you long for, you call your dream into your life!

As my friend, Author and spiritual teacher Maureen Muldoon says, "It – wanting what you have – is based on the idea that what you focus on increases." Or, as Jesus said, "So I tell you, whatever you ask for *in prayer*, believe that you have received it, and it will be yours." (Mark 11:24)

Let's say that you are an Original Romantic with a dream of becoming a Carpenter. By shifting the focus to being present to your limited abilities, as opposed to limitless abilities, soon you will be creating that mini piece of furniture, maybe a doll bed for your child, or other simple carpentry project already within you. It may be the smallest of baby steps, but that is enough. With your presence practice, the project becomes fulfilled, and you may now be ready for the next step.

Conversely, only *dreaming* of being a Carpenter or envying those who are will not get you anywhere. This seems to go without saying, but not so much for The Original Romantic. Being aware that you can be an empty dreamer, one who is unwilling to co-create, is important.

When you manage your passions of longing and envy by "telling" them that is *you who leads them in the dance* and not the other way around, you are directing your personal growth process.

The Area of Avoidance for Type Four, the Original-Romantic

The area of avoidance for Type Four, The Original Romantic is that which is ordinary or common. Original Romantics tend to avoid the usual or insignificant because they are looking to feel special. They consider anything ordinary or common to be "less than" or beneath them. Indeed, the Shakespearean quote "Mediocrity is a portion of us all" might have the most meaning for The Original Romantic.

This longing to be unique is your tendency and you work really hard at finding ways to make it a reality. This drive to both be and feel special is rooted in feelings of disconnection and abandonment of a primary caregiver. As Dr. Jerry Wagner says in his book, "The Enneagram Spectrum": "It is if Fours are searching for the Garden of Eden from which they somehow feel expelled."

Avoiding the ordinary seeps in at the low end of your type and can show up in a variety of ways, usually through a feeling of longing or envy. You think or feel that someone else has a better relationship, or home, or body, or smile, or career, or friends, and on the list goes. You may think "Why can't I be more?" Your unconscious attitude or conscious thinking, as the case may be, is about wanting to stand out. You may think that if you are special enough or extraordinary then the one who abandoned you will notice. Mega-singer-songwriter, Bruce Springsteen has lately made it public knowledge that he has experienced depression and mental illness. He manages it with helpful medication. His father also admitted to not being there for him. (Today Show November 2018.) Sometimes the greatest stars in our midst are working so very hard to be special. They have learned the root of this behavior if they are tuned in like Bruce Springsteen now is. They give us a lot in the process but at what cost to their own health?

For many Fours, it might be that a feeling of loneliness triggers this deeply rooted abandonment. These feelings can have their foundation in the first four or five years of life, when a myriad of reasons a parent or primary caregiver focuses somewhere other than you.

Original Romantic types can focus on the suffering and

longing for things the way they think they could be or should be. They entertain thoughts of, "If only my life was this way or that way," and in doing so often miss what is wonderful in your lives.

If your tendency is to avoid what is ordinary or common within you, then your task throughout your life is to find what author and Theologian John Shea calls the "sacred in the ordinary."

Triggered by something that left the Original Romantic feeling that you are not enough and disconnected from the whole, you feel the wound of abandonment.

Not liking yourself for feeling common can quickly domino down into feeling like *nothing*. This feeling of lack then may lead you to search for that ideal love or experience that is out there somewhere. This future experience will be exciting or unique in some way and will signal to you that you are indeed special.

This romantic side of the Four reminds me of Tony from *West Side Story,* who sings: "Something's coming, I don't know what it is, but it is gonna be great. The air is hummin' and something great is coming. C'mon, deliver to me." This is the Original Romantic's dreamy state of mind when he/she does not want to be in the present moment.

As an Original/Romantic, you long and yearn for *this thing*, which is coming to complete you. In this way you are a classic dreamer, and when the dream doesn't arrive the longing can turn to envy. You mourn the loss of yourself, the dream, all of it. You want what that other person has and in the meantime you miss the present moment, which is yours, all for the taking. I share this mantra with my Original Romantic clients: "I have everything I need in this moment to grow."

Remember, each type on the Enneagram has a tendency and each type has a task. Your tendency may be to look to the future to a fault, and in order to move out of this unhealthy state it is helpful to practice living in the present. For example, you might tell yourself to use your prolific imagination to find meaning in the moment, to want what you have, or to take baby steps to change what you do not want. The important point here is to take action. Little action steps at the start of a dream can lead to it being realized!

Along with this inner work and healthy self-talk to get you back to the present, it is helpful for you to name what triggered this feeling of abandonment or disconnection. Another way to move beyond this unhealthy state is to remind yourself that you are *not* abandoned. Even if this was once that case, it isn't now, and whatever triggered you to feel separation and disconnection does not have to remain a part of your experience.

It is your choice to let your old story go and create your reality, which is a full picture with you an integral part of the whole. I am not a Four, but the resourceful romantic in me knows that missing the moment, or the day, comparing myself to others is when I feel the real loss.

At the low end, when you compare yourself to others and envy them, you disconnect from your virtue of equanimity. Somewhere deep down you know and claim your equal value but when you make up this story of your lesser importance, you have forgotten your value.

It is painful for any of us to feel this way, and especially for the Original Romantic type. It feels so much healthier and integrated to believe you are a part of the whole, and that you are here to bring your unique contribution to it. It is especially important to know *that,* even when it doesn't *feel* that way.

The Wellness Map of Type Four, The Original Romantic

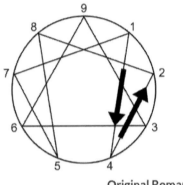

Original Romantic

The Wellness Map shows us what we feel like when we are centered and well, and what it looks like for us when we are stressed, disconnected and in varying states of dis-ease. From a psychological point of view the corresponding type you attract within when you are centered is about your integration. When you are stressed and attracting within your other corresponding type's low aspects, it is about your disintegration.

When the Type Four, Original Romantic is centered, Enneagram wisdom says you will receive gifts from Type One, The Good Reformer. That said, you get grace or gifts when you decide to center and let stress go, no matter which type on the Enneagram you fall within.

The high or resourceful side of The Good Reformer is about

integrity and seeing serenity and the perfection and wholeness in all things. It can be summed up in the adage, "Process not perfection." Actually, the process is perfect. It is both/and instead of either/or kind of thinking.

When The Original Romantic is centered, you feel that you are enough, and when you are present to a world that has enough for all of us, your connection to the world is enough. Nothing to mourn here, rather, you feel alive – you are even thriving in this connection to the whole.

Don't we all feel good when we can see the world, even in its brokenness, with this oneness potential?

The disconnected or low side of Type Four is to feel abandoned and guilty about being ordinary, even unworthy. When you are in this place, you attract within yourself the low side of Type Two, The Loving Giver and can avoid your own needs to a fault.

This manifests in the emotional passion of longing and envy going on overdrive, along with that of your false pride. Original Romantics distract themselves by helping others or meeting others' needs and avoiding their own "ordinariness." The distorted thinking here is, "I'm not worthy or good enough so I'll focus on someone else."

This disconnected Original Romantic type will martyr themselves and suffer with lack. This manifests even more feelings of sadness or depression, creating a vicious cycle of low feelings and avoidance of them. Your internalized anger at yourself builds up, leading to more depression, and a dominoing down into the gunk. It begins with unchecked feelings of disconnection (abandonment) and melancholy about something being missing, and gets contaminated with (the smokescreen of) overdrive giving. This pattern of paying more attention to others when you are in stress is about avoiding your needs because you feel you are not worth it anyway. This is clearly the absence of emotional wellness for The Original Romantic.

Knowing this pattern when you are stressed can help you navigate through this "old story" and get you back to the high side of Type One, where you realize you are enough and an integral part of the whole.

In summary, your Wellness Map as a Four, The Original or Romantic is as follows: In times of centering and safety, you are attracting within yourself the high side of Type One, The Good Reformer (you are an integral part of the whole), and in times of tension and stress you are attracting within yourself the low side of Type Two, The Loving Giver (unworthiness, martyrdom and resentment).

This is your general behavioral pattern; however, by using Enneagram wisdom and practicing healthy self-talk, we can use our new self-awareness, activate our inner GPS and do a course correction within us to new healthier behaviors. You can access the high and low side of all nine types.

The Instinctual Center of Type Four, the Original-Romantic

The preferred instinctual center of Type Four, The Original Romantic is the heart. This is where you have the most practice. In fact, the heart center is like a second skin for the Original Romantic. You feel so easily and so deeply. You are considered an Empath and are generally very intuitive.

At the low side, if you are feeling deeply, even suffering, this makes you feel a bit special. You also feel for others when they are suffering. The Four can long for and envy unattainable things, as you do not want to be a "bottom feeder." You want to be the cream that rises to the top.

When you are overly focused on standing out from the crowd, it may be helpful to remember everyone has their strengths and challenges and life is not a race.

Calming or dialing down your intense feelings is a way to open the door of truth in your head and what you know to be true in your gut before solving a problem. Solving it out of your heart center if you are on overdrive will be overly dramatic. The head and gut centers will give you the balance you need.

The Wing Style of Type Four, The Original Romantic

The wings of Type Four are Type Three, The Effective Achiever and Type Five, The Wise Observer.

If you identify with the high side of your Effective Achiever wing style, your Original Romantic personality may be influenced to put your current dreams into action. You may get the job done instead of dreaming too much about it.

If you identify with the low side of your Effective Achiever wing, you may be driven to create projects as a way to avoid feelings. You may be a chameleon and a performer. You may bottle up your feelings and then get depleted and depressed.

If you identify with the high side of The Wise Observer wing, you may manifest as a quieter and certainly less flamboyant or dramatic individual. You may be less judgmental of your feelings, and work them through in a balanced way. You might experience less angst with your feelings and manage your sensitive reactions because of your ability to draw from the big picture.

If, however, you identify with the low side of your Wise Observer wing, you may feel a need to isolate and be reclusive, but not because you don't feel worthy. Instead, you might become critical of something you've been working on, for example, your analysis of a report, and "chain yourself to your desk" in order to gather the right information. In this way you avoid intimacy and your needs.

Ways for The Type Four, The Original Romantic to Practice Balance

1. When feeling envy, longing, or the familiar "if only," practice telling yourself to want what you have. Putting attention on what's good in your life will bring more of it to you. This will make room for new ideas, and baby steps will get you closer to the dreams you want to realize.

2. Know and tell yourself that you are loved and connected already. You know this when you are tuned in. "Fake it till you make it," means practicing this self-talk, even when it might feel hollow inside. Something within will shift if you allow it to.

3. Get moving. Sweep the metaphysical or dreamy cobwebs out once a day by doing some kind of exercise. Walk the dog or hike or bike – choose something. If you can do a sport or dance that you love, even better. You will feel

better.

4. When your imagination runs wild with melancholy, turn it in the direction of positive action steps to get closer to the dream that you long for. Try writing one idea or action step, then two, then three, and as many as you can. Take your time with this. Give it fifteen minutes.

   Another way is to choose the fast pen method, writing down anything and everything even if it seems silly, because you may get a few good ideas towards actualizing your dream.

5. Know that creative energy begets creative energy. Begin. Stop. Begin again. When you stop or slow, say, "Thank you for the space." Say, and believe, "The rest is as important as the work." Be okay with the rest part. It is not a race. If you practice enjoying your rest stops in the creative process, you make room for a new dynamic to come forth.

6. Say, "I have everything I need in this moment to grow." Even if it doesn't feel like it, you will open the space for something to manifest. This self-talk is an act of faith.

7. Find the sacred in the ordinary. Did you ever see someone tripping out on marijuana, how they love and laugh about each and every little thing? I'm not recommending a drug- induced fantasy here, just the idea that you go somewhere and naturally trip out. Look up at the clouds and find animal and human shapes that are so clear, like a baby playing with an angel and a dog. Look at a blade of grass and trip out on how many there are in your yard, or how many petals there are in a hydrangea

or the perfect symmetry of a daisy, or a rose. Look around. Find the extraordinary everywhere.

8. Know that we are all works in progress, ever evolving. Feel the freedom in that.

9. When feeling of disconnection (old abandonment wounds and tapes) creep in, find a friend to talk with or a coach to get you back to center. Often the reconnection just takes hearing from, and being heard, by one person.

10. Remember that you bring so much to the table – sensitivity, compassion, intuition, and a flair for the beautiful and the creative. The world needs those gifts, so stop beating yourself up for being overly sensitive. You are working to manage and direct those intense feelings into actions that will make a difference in the world. Remember that raising your vibration raises everything else around you.

CHAPTER FIVE

Type Five, The Wise Observer

"Sharing heart experiences will influence a more complete body mind spirit way of knowing."

A Short Story of a Wise Observer

One of my favorite comments came from a friend who is a Wise Observer: "I love my wife and daughter very much; sometimes I just feel closer to them when I'm in the other room."

I laughed out loud when I heard that; it must have resonated somewhere within me too!

We all know what it is like to be safe within the corners of our cave, whether we are Wise Observers or not. This is evidenced by the term, "man-cave," which has become part of our common vernacular. Women decided they would like a woman-cave too, only they called it a "she-shed." As we will see, man-caves and she-sheds can be real or metaphorical, and they are a place Wise Observers go to be in solitude and collect information.

My friend was being funny, and even poking fun at himself, but it begs the question; when he talks about putting space between himself and those he loves, is he making a healthy choice or is he being stingy or withholding with his feelings and thoughts because he looks upon his family members as intrusions to his space?

He doesn't feel good about being withholding, or "invisible," even though he seems to prefer it. What a paradox! And within every Enneagram type there is a paradox of our tendencies and our tasks or inner awareness work. In fact, his making a joke about it is actually healthy because it points to his awareness of his issue.

When he stays in his cave, real or metaphorical, collecting the information that fills him up, he moves away from people. He misses out on real interpersonal connection, which he knows deep down has equal if not more importance in his life than his tendency to remain alone in his quests.

His metaphorical cave is a place where he withholds himself with such comments, as "Yes, dear," appearing as if he is listening to his wife while tuning her out. He can also appear stand off-ish or even cold. It can be a turn-off to people when he acts like this, which is what he wants when he is disconnected, or beside himself.

He may turn down invitations to connect and share dinner or something fun with people.

He may spin his wheels between collecting information and scattered thinking like,

"This is not enough," and so he looks for more information, and on and on it goes.

When this friend, who is a brilliant Wise Observer, is decidedly better, that is, more connected to his heart, he comes out of that cave, for he knows it can keep him from experiencing life. He connects to his feelings, and shares from his heart, even if that means making jokes about himself, which he often does. He shows himself to be self-aware, and he is clear about how important personal connections are to his growth. He shares his feelings and wisdom with me and he is clear, sensitive and assertive. When he shares like that, we both feel not only more enlightened but authentic and empowered as well.

The Strengths and Challenges of Type Five, The Wise Observer

Strengths that The Wise Observer brings to the table:

Good Analyzer

Sees big picture

Smart/scholarly

Contained

Insightful

About the truth

Funny/witty

Transparent

Non-judgemental

Empowering

Challenges that The Wise Observer brings to the table.

Hermit-like

Distracted

Commitment-phobic

Procrastinates

Sits on sidelines

Avoids feelings

Withholding

Non-relational

Unavailable

Snobby or cold

Overly-Academic

The Emotional Passion of Type Five, the Wise Observer

The emotional passion or driving energy of The Wise Observer is avarice. The definition of avarice, or greed, is an insatiable desire for wealth or gain. This is not necessary financial, however; in fact, it is more often a greed for information, space, or time.

If you are a Wise Observer, greed is what you feel when you are stressed. It can happen when you feel tension rising and this is when you may lock the door to your cave, figuratively or literally. Said differently, this greed is an unwillingness to share yourself.

Individual space can serve all of us, but the passion of avarice or greed on overdrive is different from healthy space. It is isolating yourself from your own feelings or the feelings of others.

Passions are like programs that hum along within us, that make us tick. In terms of colors, think of passions in gradations from pale pink to fiery red. Our passions are always with us, as long as we are living in a body. They are not easy to turn off but you can learn to dial them down and lead them in your dance, so to speak.

A self-awareness and self-mastery process is about knowing that your passion is operating and that you are managing it to the best of your conscious ability. When your passion is growing in its intensity alongside a problem or challenge, this is the time to take note of it.

What does it look like to be greedy with yourself? It can manifest as a withholding of your feelings or giving the "cold shoulder" to another. It can show up as staying in your office or room too long or hiding behind a computer screen or a TV. It can look like a spouse complaining to you that her feelings are not really heard.

You can be greedy with yourself even when you are with people because you are in observation mode, that is, watching and seeing instead of being seen and sharing. When you are greedy with yourself you are often "invisible."

Greed of the self happens when there is a lack of connection to your heart. Getting a handle on the emotional passion of avarice or greed will include getting in touch with what you are feeling, and being generous with yourself in exploring all of your feelings. Each day, each hour, it is good practice to check in with yourself and ask how you feel about something, even if it seems inconsequential. In soul-searching, you use the entire keyboard of feelings.

When you share freely with yourself, the feelings of others won't make you so anxious. You won't feel the need to let the passion of greed run you, or go on "automatic," as Helen Palmer calls it. It is helpful to use your great observational talents to watch all forms of avarice or greed within you. Are you greedy in other ways besides with your feelings? It is a good question for reflection for all Enneagram types, but especially The Wise Observer.

Certainly sharing yourself is not always in order, but Enneagram awareness and practice means looking at when you are being managed by your passion. In this deepened awareness you use your observational skills on yourself. This awareness helps you manage yourself. With practice you can slow down the automatic train and create responses rather than reactions. Good emotional health is ultimately about balance within.

Remember that like the other passions, greed is not "bad" in and of itself. Being greedy with yourself is why you can be contained, a voracious reader, and a wise observer; it is only when it goes on overdrive or out of balance that it becomes unhealthy. Ask yourself, "Am I isolating myself too much? Can I notice when I get over-satiated with information to the exclusion of my primary relationships?" These are good self-reflection questions that will deepen your connections to what you are feeling.

The Area of Avoidance of Type Five, The Wise Observer

The area of avoidance – or blind spot – for The Wise Observer is a fear or being emptied out. Filling up is, for example, reading and collecting information, the more the better. As an "Ivory Tower" type who likes to learn, you have worked hard to become observational and collecting all that information takes a long time. If someone wants to talk with you or tries to be social when you are tense or stressed, your information-gathering time will likely feel intruded upon. Gathering information tends to feel satiating to you more than a lot of heart-to-heart talks.

A person may press you to share from your heart, but when you are in stress that kind of sharing is difficult because you are still trying to figure out what your heart's information is about.

This is a challenge for you, however, because you like to receive data in a neat, clean manner, and as we all know the heart space can be messy.

To have feelings unloaded before you have analyzed and processed them may feel threatening to you. Hoarding thoughts, time, space and information can seem like a guarantee against feeling emptied out, but this pattern moves you away from your heart space, which is the area that needs attention.

Remember the emotional passion or program that runs for the Wise Observer is greed of the self. You have a tendency to stay in your head and avoid emotions and people who want to get close to you. You are comfortable in your head. You get prickly in your heart space and, feeling drained from emotion you withhold and revert to your cave, real or metaphorical. You like to call the shots and feel the need to dole yourself out.

The healthier you are emotionally, and the more self-aware,

you will understand your antisocial behavior pattern, and in doing so, understand the need to connect with people. Connecting more with others will bring you into balance and begin to feel increasingly gratifying.

The Wellness Map of Type Five, The Wise Observer

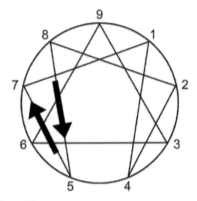

Wise Observer

When centered and safe, The Wise Observer receives or attracts to his/her interior life the high side of Type Eight, The Powerful Protector. When you are stressed or disconnected from yourself and your feelings, you receive from or attract within the low side of Type Seven, The Joyful Adventurer.

When you are centered, you stay with and share what is in your heart. You also share your knowledge, wisdom, time, space, and energy, realizing it empowers yourself and others. Mother Teresa said, "Do small things with great love." This can apply to how Wise Observers share. Stretching yourself with the best intentions can mean a lot. Making the effort to connect counts here.

When you're operating from the high side, you find out that instead of feeling empty or intruded upon, you can actually feel satisfied and full from sharing on an intimate basis; you may even feel proud of yourself, which is exactly the opposite of what you were avoiding in the state of tension or stress. You call in to yourself the gifts of equanimity and true empowerment from Type Eight.

On the low side, you believe that if you share too much of your time, energy, or resources you will get depleted. When you feel tension rising and are stressed, your tendency to go invisible gets activated. To stay invisible from yourself you shield yourself from your feelings as well as withholding yourself from others. It is here where you receive from the low side of Seven and scatter in a hundred directions; you feel the need to collect more information or experiences.

Your journey back to well-being begins with your awareness of your patterns of greed of self and fear of feelings, and an understanding of how to get out of your own way when this behavior is self-defeating. You may shift this unhealthy behavior by telling yourself, "I am going on automatic again, this is not what I want to be doing here. I am getting scattered, because I am afraid of feeling. If I slow down this train, I see that I can handle sharing on this feeling level and I know deep down it makes me feel better somehow. I have observed complacency and it is not what I am going for here. I am going for growth."

Self-talk of this nature can assist us all, but especially The Wise Observer.

When I write about the Wellness Map, I become acutely aware of our tendencies and our tasks. Rumi said it best: "Your task is not to seek for love, but merely to seek and find all the barriers within yourself that you have built against it."

As a Wise Observer, your Wellness Map will show you states of well-being and states of unease. Your ability to enlighten or unburden and see the big picture of things, as well as your ability to empower others with that wisdom, is your place of wellness, your kind of heaven on earth.

Your withholding, hoarding, scattering and splintering to hold onto more information or whatever, can feel like a kind of hell on earth. This is the kind of hell where you get in a deep way that you've been imprisoned by your habitual patterns and long to be free. This aha moment may help you to break out of your ivory tower and feel alive more often.

In summary, the Wellness Map for The Wise Observer is as follows: When you are centered (secure, safe) you are attracting within yourself the high side of Type Eight, The Powerful Protector type. It is the combination of navigating through your knowledge *and* your feelings that you find your balance and your power. In turn you help others own theirs.

In times of tension and stress you are attracting within yourself the low side of Type Seven, the Joyful Adventurer. Scattering for more information and splintering out avoiding feelings and emptiness. This is your general behavioral pattern.

Remember, *you can* access the high side and low side of all of the nine types on the spectrum.

The Instinctual Center of Type Five, The Wise Observer

The head is the dominant instinctual center for The Wise Observer; in fact, it could be said that they are the ultimate head type on the Enneagram spectrum. The Five is comfortable collecting information; they find it soothing, the way talking can be for a Seven, (Joyful Adventurer) or seeing all sides of a story is for a Nine (Peaceful Mediator). Collecting information and more, (think collecting wood and then splitting it, and then stacking it and collecting more, now repeat etc…) whether you are reading it from a book, newspaper, magazine, or off a computer, or alone, observing – not participating – at a cocktail party or alone on the streets, acts as insulation from the outside world, or more specifically the people in your world. Observers fill up on seeing, that is, observations, getting information, getting satisfied the way The Loving Giver gets "full" from giving.

The problem isn't with your great capacity to collect and retain the knowledge you collect. That is a given. This is about the Wise Observer's good emotional health, or balance. It is about when your interest in observing, learning and gathering information overshadows and maybe even replaces your relationships. Getting familiar with these patterns in yourself and being present to them will be helpful in checking in with yourself, in an honest and intimate way. A healthy Five can ask, "Am I out of balance in my relationships?" They can also ask the same question to their loved ones.

Put your hands over your heart and ask yourself if you are hiding out. If your answer is yes, what specifically is causing this behavior at this time? With heart-motivated self-reflection and discernment time, you can hear your inner wisdom.

Check in with your gut too; that is, use your great observational powers to witness the sensations that your feelings cause in your body. Name them, i.e., what is the need behind the fear or anger? Stay with yourself to work them through the way you would stay with a research paper or another project that requires discipline.

The Wing Style of Type Five, The Wise Observer

The Wing styles of Type Five, The Wise Observer are Type Four, The Original Romantic and Type Six, The Loyal Skeptic.

If you are a Wise Observer and you identify with the high side of your Original Romantic wing, you may be more feeling and even more tuned in to your deep feelings. You may be an original thinker, one who has a fine aesthetic, and is less detached generally and more sensitive.

If you identify with the low side of Four, you may feel overly emotional and moody or disappointed in people, and, deciding you don't want anything to do with anyone, you hide out in your cave.

If you identify with the high side of your Loyal Skeptic wing, you may move more toward people, than away from them, and not see them as intrusive when they share their feelings with you. You may want to make contact with others, especially those to whom you feel a loyalty. Your loyalty to yourself may manifest by your being more accepting of your feelings.

If you identify with low side of your Six, you may be even more cautious in your thinking.

Your doubting Thomas attitude may lead you to second-guess and even mistrust others, as well as much of what you read or research. You may also mistrust yourself, which leads to overdoing things. This has been called analysis-paralysis, meaning, for example, you do not know when it is time to sign your work.

Ways for Type Five, The Wise Observer to Practice Balance

1. Remind yourself that no one really has the Big Picture, or will ever have it, so you can rest from searching for it all the time. Instead, relax a little and have a good time with others.

2. When you are not contributing much to the conversations you are in, and sitting on the sidelines literally or metaphorically, ask yourself two questions:

    "Am I being withholding?" and "Is that how I would like to be perceived?" If you are withdrawing and being reclusive, you know you need to listen to your own heart more and move toward, not away, from the person.

3. If tension starts to rise and you feel anxious about sharing from your heart, and you find yourself retreating to your head and your cave or both, breathe into this thought: "Experience with others is a great teacher." Then remind yourself to share conversations with just one person, or enjoy a shared experience such as a movie where there is deep characterization and then talk about it afterwards. Do anything except something that requires you to collect information individually.

4. When you feel yourself overthinking something and the monkey mind starts running, exercise your body in some way. A walk or a bike ride can clear your head and help you to "see" the solution to a problem more effectively than collecting more data can.

5. One of your assets is your ability to be clear in your communications. Get clear in your own self-observations

and self-talk. Know that as a Five, you will always have a tendency to move away from the group. Ask yourself what is the worst that can happen if you move toward someone with affection or a feeling statement.

6. When you feel that you will be drained by others or that they will cause you to feel empty or just "worse," in general, and you feel a strong desire to read or go to the computer, remind yourself that it is good for you to reach out and connect with a real person.

7. When you are scattering and splintering yourself with too many isolated intellectual projects or pursuits, slow down, and remind yourself that less can be more.

8. Have a regular time for socializing, whether it be a monthly book group discussion, a weekly movie night and dinner, or a morning walking group. Walking and talking can go together nicely. If you find yourself thinking, "Oh I do not like to do those things," try something more palatable. If your tendency is to move away from people, you need to work on moving toward them in a way that involves some depth of feeling.

9. When you share your heart wisdom, as well as your knowledge, with others you own your power and teach them to own theirs.

10. Remember you have a great capacity for being understanding; non-judgmentally seeing the bigger picture; and practicing healthful detachment or non-attachment. This is especially helpful to those of us who can get reactive, and sharing these qualities rather than hoarding them will set an example for others and empower them too.

CHAPTER SIX

Type Six, The Loyal Skeptic

"Remember that concern proceeds with caution, fear paralyzes." —Neale Donald Walsh

A Short Story of a Loyal Skeptic

"Trust no one."

While the above adage is a bit of a caricature of the Loyal Skeptic type, I would contend that a very self-aware Six would agree that they have a tendency to be vigilant thinkers and questioning types. At the high or healthy side of The Loyal Skeptic, this vigilance might look like, "I need to pay careful attention and question this situation." If they are in a more stressful place it might be colored as, "You cannot trust what you see." Ironically, some Loyal Skeptics I know often say "trust me" when sharing advice, but they may find it difficult to trust or to have faith in themselves or others.

There was a woman in one of my introductory Enneagram classes who doubted the information. I rarely have this reaction from students, though sometimes it takes a while for them to process the information. While I was fleshing out the Enneagram types, this particular student said, quite vehemently, "I don't like systems that put people in boxes."

I reassured her that the purpose of the Enneagram was not to put people in a box, but rather to make you very aware of the survival box (ego) you set up to cope with life when you were very young. The Enneagram's wisdom is time-honored because it motivates you and me to stretch from the survival box to a box of thriving. In this thriving box, you could take down the box's walls and learn new healthier ways of living and loving and connecting to your center more often.

I added that Enneagram wisdom absolutely teaches that you are more than your personality. The spiritual practice of the Enneagram helps you connect your personality to your spirit. There are many transformational practices, and the Enneagram is one of them.

Whatever our Enneagram personality type, when we react on automatic it is indicative that we are in survival mode. We may be comfortable in a habitual kind of way, but we are not centered when we react from old patterns that do not work for us. This woman felt neither safe nor centered as far as I could see. As a result of her "Doubting Thomas" patterns, she did not trust me, or the information that I was sharing. She was really being led by her doubt and fear instead of her faith. I had a strong intuition that she was a type Six, The Loyal Skeptic, and from her tone and her statement I knew I would have to earn her trust.

The happy ending to this teacher student story was that I did indeed earn her trust, and she became more aware of her tendency to mistrust anything that seemed out of her norm. She even admitted she was working on self-awareness with regard to her mistrustful way. She admitted that she could lash out during these times, a counter-phobic reaction like that of a scared dog who bites.

She was very interested to learn strategies that would help her feel more centered and open to trusting others and situations, instead of looking for what could go wrong. She wanted more often to tap into her intuition (strong inner knowing) rather than overanalyzing situations. She worked at this and worked at trusting herself, so that the adage "To Thine Own Self Be True" developed new meaning and value for her. The Enneagram's wisdom and her personal map for her personality Type Six helped her gain a new clarity and calm.

The Strengths and Challenges of Type Six, The Loyal Skeptic

Strengths that The Loyal Skeptic brings to the table:

Faithful

Loyal

Steadfast

Strong inner knowing

Hardworking

Traditional

Debunks false authority

Vigilant

Circumspect

Prepared

Challenges that The Loyal Skeptic Brings to the table:

Doubting Thomas behavior

Mistrustful

Negative

Vigilante

Catastrophic-thinking

Black and white thinking

Nervous Nellie

Close minded

Overly fearful

Tense

The Emotional Passion of Type Six, The Loyal Skeptic

The emotional passion of Type Six, The Loyal Skeptic is fear and doubt. It is a kind of dread that, "If something can go wrong it will." This fear state manifests mainly as phobic or counter-phobic. An example of phobic is the rabbit in the yard, twitching and vigilant and outright scared. An example of counter-phobic would be the aggressively barking dog, who has been pacing the fence. The dog is scared of the neighbor's loud lawnmower, but is presenting as mad. This driving energy of fear runs similar programs in each Loyal Skeptic to one degree or another.

Fear can be a good thing, such as when a truck is coming at high speed around the corner that you happen to be standing on. It is when fear runs you all over town with a ring in your nose that you need to change the dynamic and direct it. Think, "Do I need you now, fear, doubt or angst, or no?"

Knowing what trouble spots can look like when the emotional passion is on overdrive can help you to manage or direct the passion into its proper place. Trouble spots are not limited to but include overanalyzing or obsessing about a situation, scanning the environment for what could go wrong, or immediately mistrusting someone when they haven't really given you reason to at that point. Another sign of being in need of balance is when you have an angry outburst which seems to come from out of nowhere, or stiffening up in a rigid manner.

When these traits surface and you find yourself stressed, naming the passion and breathing into it will slow down the train of the emotion. You might say to yourself, "Okay, I am so on fear/worry/doubt/angst overdrive." Naming it takes the edge off of the emotions sharpness almost immediately. You can do a vigilance test to help you identify and become familiar with what this overdrive looks like. Ask yourself:

- What would the best outcome be right now?

- Am I making a mountain out of a molehill?

- Am I cultivating stinking thinking?

- Am I just being a Nervous Nellie because of old stories

and patterns?

- Can I see how these old patterns do not serve me anymore?

- Am I feeding my faith and starving my fears (because they need no feeding)

- Is this new experience not trustworthy just because it is out of my norm?

- Do I believe deep down that my Source is with me, not against me?

- Can I get out of my head and into my body center (my gut) and hear my guidance?

The Area of Avoidance for Type Six, The Loyal Skeptic

"You cannot trust what you see; even sugar looks like salt."

The area of avoidance – or blind spot – for Type Six, The Loyal Skeptic is deviance. If a behavior, person or situation seems "out there" or outside the norm, the stressed Loyal Skeptic will look it over. If she is not aware of her tendency to avoid things that seem different, she may magnify the potential problems within. She may have catastrophic thinking, such as, "If I give my child too much freedom, she will participate in deviant behaviors that I am opposed to." A Loyal Skeptic in a stressful situation will have a tendency to see all of the negatives.

A conversation with Loyal Skeptic might go like this: You say, "Can we not give equal time to the possible positive outcome here, instead of always dwelling and speculating on the irrational hazards that are to come?"

If you are a Healthy Six, you're aware that in a stressful situation you have the tendency to avoid anything out of your norm or "box," but you can catch yourself more often. You can say, and mean, "What might the best outcome be?" You can use your vigilance to see different sides of a situation and this may calm you.

The Wellness Map of Type Six, The Loyal Skeptic

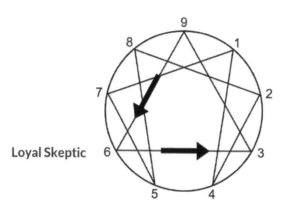

When a Loyal Skeptic is centered, you receive from or attract within the gifts and grace from Type Nine, The Peaceful Mediator. When you are tense or stressed, you receive from the low side of Type Three, The Effective Achiever.

When you center yourself with feelings of calm and clarity, you feel a true happiness. You have made a choice to hear and trust your own wisdom. You use your skill of being dependable and you turn that inward to rely on yourself. You are clear about your ability to problem solve because you have chosen to let go of the doubts and fears that can follow you around like a puppy waiting to be fed.

You use your great ability to play the devil's advocate with your fears. You lean into the fear, observing it, not running from it, because you know if you deny it, it will control you.

Your skeptical and questioning mind can find balance with a knowing that you do not always have to have proof in order to trust something. If the idea you originally mistrust feels right and helps a situation, that can be proof enough. When you use your common sense, combined with your intuition to balance an overactive mind, your Loyal Skeptic personality can put the second-guessing to rest, find its inner trust and peaceful qualities.

Getting familiar with something or someone always brings a kind of comfort so it is good to get familiar with your fears and your anxiety's voice. With this practice of leaning in and ob-serving doubts, fears and second-guessing, you can catch your-self.

Would you would rather you spend your time scanning the environment for trouble, or being present to the joy around you? If you choose the latter, it is time to send your inner doubting Thomas packing.

When you are centered, you may ask *why not* instead of *why?* You reassure yourself with what you already know deep inside: that life is big and wide and can have many different interpretations and your vigilance can never capture all of it.

You only need to have your own experience. You need not project on to others your own experience or mix up their experience with yours. Trusting yourself is easier said than done, and it is the task of the ever-questioning mind of the Loyal Skeptic. When you are loyal to yourself, in your careful way, you are *knowing*. This very trust of yourself creates a calm, which attracts the gifts of Type Nine, The Peaceful Mediator within. You are now peaceful instead of frantic, filled with second-guessing and static.

When The Loyal Skeptic is stressed out, you get your doubt and fear program up and attract the low side of Type Three, The Effective Achiever, which can include making your image or role more important than your feelings and truth.

A friend who falls under Type Six, The Loyal Skeptic called me one day and asked, "Where do I go again when I am stressed?" I said, "It starts with second-guessing yourself, then it's like you look for ways to find an answer until you wear yourself out with overdoing to please others. " She said "That's exactly what I am doing and I am going to stop it right now." I said, "You have your answer within you, trust it."

When you are not aware of your resistance to deviance, that is, anything that would be out of your rule-following comfort zone, or you are not aware of your devil's advocate stance (either being rebellious or authority-consciousness, you can let doubt and fear run the show). Said differently, when you are aware of these stances of resistance, either a resistance to anything *but* authority or the other extreme of questioning and resisting *any* authority, you can better work through your fears.

This is easier said than done when your anxieties have anxieties, however, meditation, breath work and self-talk can help slow down the catastrophic train and calm states of anxiety and fear.

As you get further along in your own self-awareness and emotional health process, there will be times when you never even let this worry train start.

As my sister has often said in a tense moment, "I'm not going to crazy land."

Writing down what you are worried about or discussing it with a trusted person can be an effective tool in slowing down a racing fearful mind. Another great strategy that I have learned for anxiety is this: If anxiety persists, give it the floor for five minutes, not a second more. Then get moving, exercise will often melt anxiety like butter in a hot pan.

Self-mastery and staying in states of wellbeing, where you are calm and clear, is not only possible but probable with practice. It is here where The Loyal Skeptic is in her truest states of k-*now*-ing.

In summary, the Wellness Map for The Loyal Skeptic is as follows: In times of centering and safety, you are attracting within yourself the high side of Type Nine, The Peaceful Mediator type (clarity and calm with effective harmony in action), and in times of tension and stress you are attracting within yourself the low side of Type Three, The Effective Achiever (avoidance of feelings and overdoing).

This is your general behavioral pattern. Remember, *you can* access the high side and low side of all of the nine types on the spectrum.

The Instinctual Center of Type Six, The Loyal Skeptic

The head is the dominant instinctual center for the Loyal Skeptic, which explains why he/she is analytical, prepared, thoughtful, and has great attention to detail.

Sixes can fill up on scanning the environment for what

might go wrong, and it is when your over-vigilance gets coupled with your overthinking that you lose balance and feel disconnected from your harmony and peace. In times of stress these worries and fears can multiply and one butterfly can turn into a swarm of them. A little thing that others might not even notice can become a potential catastrophe for the stressed Loyal Skeptic.

The second-guessing and overthinking can drive you to work even harder and to seek approval and please others. It is especially in such times that you need to check in with your heart for the compassion it can bring. The heart center will calm your head and bring you to a truer knowing. Likewise, when you check in with your gut center, the information there will underline your true knowing. It is in your body that you can know the answers to your dilemmas by way of the body's many sensations, which are produced by the thoughts and feelings.

The Wing Style of Type Six, The Loyal Skeptic

The wing styles for The Loyal Skeptic are Type Five, The Wise Observer and Type Seven, The Joyful Adventurer, one of which has a dominant role.

A Loyal Skeptic type with a Wise Observer wing may be more reserved and introverted than a Loyal Skeptic with a Joyful Adventurer wing. If as a Loyal Skeptic you identify with the higher aspects of your Five wing, your reserved way will not rob you of your ability to connect with others in a meaningful way. You may be well equipped to have heart-to-heart talks with others. You may hear what your own heart is saying to you and be more apt to work through your feelings, because a healthy Five knows that hearing and processing feelings is a way to achieve wisdom and balance.

Loyal Skeptics with a Wise Observer wing will be very interested in their truth, as healthy Sixes are, and if you identify with the high side of the Wise Observer, you may also find yourself less judgmental and less interested in seeking approval from others. Others' attitudes and perspectives may seem less interesting.

Also, your ability to see the big picture, coupled with The Wise Observer wing's influence, may help you get in touch with your own inner perspective. This can be very helpful for the Six who has a tendency to second-guess themselves and/or doubt others.

If the Six identifies with the low side of The Wise Observer wing, you might become more reclusive, disconnected, and doubt others more. As you mistrust your feelings and live from an overactive mind, you may over consume information, intellectualize or fantasize. You may scatter and splinter out, getting too many projects going at once. You may hoard newly found, or even rehashed information.

If as a Loyal Skeptic you identify with the high side of the Joyful Adventurer wing, you may often be more extroverted, chattier and personable, rather than reserved. The positivity of The Joyful Adventurer wing may influence you to better keep your doubts and fears in check. The Joyful Adventurer's childlike tendency to leap before looking can actually help The Loyal Skeptic find yourself jumping in to a situation with courage instead of fear.

If The Loyal Skeptic identifies with the lower side of Seven, your thinking may get scattered instead of focused. Your need to be vigilant and scan for information may double in size. A gluttonous and rigid self-critical factor may go on overdrive and keep you from trusting yourself. In this stressful state you may consume too much, in a myriad of ways that could include eating, shopping, drinking or planning.

Ways For Type Six, The Loyal Skeptic to Practice Balance

1. Ask yourself, "What is the best outcome here?" Give equal time to those thoughts, not just the worst-case scenarios, when feeling irrational mistrust.

2. When tension is rising and you feel yourself beginning to doubt or not trust a situation or a person, check in with your gut and ask what its guidance is. Pay attention to bodily cues like a jittery sensation in your belly.

3. "Keep an open mind" is a mantra made for The Loyal Skeptic. When rigid thinking is your main mode of operating, it is time to give yourself a pep talk about all the people who accomplished great things in history by keeping an open mind. Practice both/and thinking instead of being suspicious.

4. Remind yourself each day that the force is with us, not against us.

5. When you feel a drive toward busy-ness or overdoing, slow the train down and tell yourself, "Quality not quantity." Spinning your wheels is not the goal. Your inner knowing will recognize how you are distracting yourself with projects when you are anxious, and it will

be a relief to slow down or stop.

6. When you find yourself lashing out at someone because you are in a state of fear, doubt or mistrust, ask yourself if you have given them the benefit of the doubt.

7. Feel it to heal it. When you are in your head too much, you cannot be an effective problem solver. Hold onto the uncomfortable feeling long enough to identify it. If it is anxiety, slowing things down, rather than speeding things up, will help you work through it.

8. Instead of saying "What if?", practice saying "So what?" If you read this and say "That just isn't me," remember everything can get better with practice.

9. Each day cultivate your courageous side by doing one thing you fear doing.

10. One of your greatest gifts is your ability to be loyal and faithful to yourself and your loved ones.

CHAPTER SEVEN

Type Seven, The Joyful Adventurer

"Focus is your holy work. Presence is your gift to yourself and others."

A Short Story of a Joyful Adventurer

Once upon a time, when a Joyful Adventurer was little, it seemed everyone saw the light in her eyes. This light was bright and when their own light was dim, they wanted hers. They found if they hung around her or held her close or played her toddler games with her, the light spread out to them. Her light was that big and could do that. They never meant to hurt her while wanting her to share that light; it was just a natural response to want to lift their mood too.

They always left her presence feeling a bit lighter and happier. And so the pattern of spreading the light went for the little girl. Pretty soon the little girl could see how she brightened up the lives of others by just being her joyful, happy-go-lucky self.

One of her favorite TV characters was Tinkerbell and she was in fact a lot like her! The little girl grew up having lots of friends to have fun with and to be a good friend to in sad times, but sad times were especially sad and hard for the Joyful Adventurer, so she would find a way how to lift herself out of them. Like Tinkerbell, she always found a light in another experience to immerse herself in when she needed.

Through her school days she continued to have friends to have fun with and was popular with the boys too and never lacked for any attention from them. People told her she was pretty and had a great smile and vivaciousness. One year she was even invited to four special dances, which included neighboring high schools! She was happy but deep down did not always have the confidence that is earned from having to prove yourself with hard work or effort and patience. She yearned for this confidence, which she saw in certain adults she knew.

The yearning grew, until one day during her freshman year at college, this lack of confidence and sadness was all she could think of or feel. She felt very small at a very big time in her life. She was so filled with sadness and criticism of herself for feeling like a failure in her nursing program that she just fell apart. She cried and felt exhaustion fill her in the guidance counselor's office.

The doctor she saw called it a depression and an identity crisis. Many kids her age were experimenting with drugs or traveling to find themselves. She, however, would go the route of intense therapy. Somewhere in her mixed up self was a strong young woman who could do and be anything she wanted to be. Her essence was calling her and she was remembering it!

With trust in her wonderful therapist, her inner work had begun. She no longer had to push down feelings or run from them when they got scary, and stay in her head.

In fact her head felt like it was exploding from all the over-thinking she was doing. In exploring all of her emotions, fears, doubts, about young adulthood and the transition it entailed, she learned that in order to heal she would have to feel.

This Joyful Adventurer had begun the best adventure of her life, the adventure of inner work. At the end of her three months of hard work in therapy, she began to feel a good deal better. Though she still had the insecurities common in young adulthood, she would deal with them instead of running onto something else like she had done as a young girl or in high school.

Her ordeal taught her that developing self-awareness and self-esteem, her emotional wellness would forever be a priority in her life.

The following year she felt clear about going back to school, as she now had a better knowing of her strengths and talents. She went onto have a meaningful career and wonderful marriage and family. Most importantly, she knew the gifts that can come from pain and limits, and from that experience she learned about her ability to focus and to have great discipline. This made her feel a deep confidence about herself, and she was extremely grateful for her newfound health.

The Strengths and Challenges of Type Seven, the Joyful Adventurer

Strengths that The Joyful Adventurer brings to the table:

Enthusiastic

Grateful

Optimistic

Vivacious

Popular

Charismatic

Fun and Funny

Personable

Warm-hearted

Non-judgmental

Challenges that The Joyful Adventurer brings to the table:

Scattered, splintered

Distracted

Gets allota-much running

Overly high expectations

Ungrounded

Jackie of all trades

Spread too thin

Critical of self, others

Impulsive

"Me first"

The Emotional Passion of Type Seven, The Joyful Adventurer

For The Joyful Adventurer, the emotional passion is gluttony. Though the word gluttony usually brings to mind an overindulgence in food, there is actually much more to it, no pun intended. Gluttony can be over-indulgence of any kind. It can be spending too much time on the computer or cellular phone, or over-planning. Perhaps the most important thing I have learned as a Seven is that gluttony is the opposite of focus and presence.

Like any other emotional passion, gluttony, when managed, adds flavor to your personality.

Enneagram practice helps you catch yourself when your passion is managing you, and helps you get back to your essence, where you are really meant to be.

To direct the emotional passion of gluttony is to notice and slow down your reaction and compulsion towards "a lotta much." It is helpful when managing your passion of gluttony to name and work the area you have a tendency to avoid, which are, limits.

As a Seven, when I work through this blind spot and give it a name (i.e. feeling limited), I get a handle on what "I do" in these limiting painful moments. I realize my tendency is to distract, gluttonize on something, or over-plan. Certainly while in this state I am not living in the present moment. I am also not present when I let my passion of gluttony race past my feelings when I rush to get to the next thrill. I am letting gluttony make the call when I run past someone else's feelings because they call up a kind of discomfort in me. You may have heard, "Do not walk ahead of me or behind me, just alongside me." Staying with their own and another's feelings, painful though they may be, is part of the critical task of the Seven.

It shows the focus and staying power of the Joyful Adventurer.

When I am centered, I feel no compulsion to run, distract, or plan. I can *stay* with the feeling of being limited and observe myself. I can stop the pull to distract myself in a myriad of ways.

In the practice of becoming aware of my frustration with limits, the passion of gluttony loses its grip on me. Sevens like the light and stimulation and excitement. Being stifled or limited doesn't always initially feel good, but it can feel like a portal to your deeper self.

When you are aware of your blind spot of avoiding limits and can be present to stay with it despite your emotional discomfort you can see how much stronger you feel. If you work it through instead of running to replace it with distraction then you feel in tune with your deeper self.

We all experience the lower and higher aspects of each of the nine types. When we want to avoid or run from limits or anything that is "not fun," we are experiencing what the Seven experiences when the blind spot or area of avoidance is activated. Sevens can experience FOMO, or Fear of Missing

Out. Distraction is a smokescreen for the avoidance of emotional pain and/or limits.

You tell yourself that you are fine, perhaps that you're even managing it, when in fact you are neither. What you are is scattered, with a racing mind. Sevens, when stressed, walk in a cloud of "the more hurried I go, the behind-er I get."

I remember several occasions when my busy young family was trying to get out of the house to some event. It always felt rushed and stressful to me. That would be the time I would notice another household task to tend to. My son Chris would say, "Mom, why do you do that? We gotta go or we'll be late!" Since I have cultivated my deepened awareness with my Enneagram type I know why I do this and can better manage the need for distraction when I am feeling stress.

Emotionally healthy Sevens work on your tendency to avoid limits and instead embrace them. You practice presence, painful or not, because it leads you to your bigger picture which is much more grounded, satisfying, and filled with grace.

The Area of Avoidance of Type Seven, The Joyful Adventurer

"Psychic pain pushes until it pulls."

As mentioned in the previous section, the area of avoidance for The Joyful Adventurer is limits. Ignoring something painful doesn't really solve it, and pushing away things that your spirit wants you to notice and work through only increases their intensity. Like a pile that gets pushed under the rug so you don't have to see it, it is still there. So too your perceived limit that causes you pain and frustration will remain when you ignore it or push it down. It grows as it continues to be swept into that same pile under the rug.

Being stifled or limited doesn't feel good initially, but it can and will feel gratifying as you go into the deeper realms of your true self.

When you are aware of your blind spot – that is, your avoidance of limits and boundaries – you are noticing your lack of patience. Practicing patience is a critical piece in the Seven's emotional growth because they want to move through discomfort *now*! It is frustrating for you when you would prefer to fly through the challenge, and it takes days, months, or even years to work through the task at hand. Naming and being in touch with this frustration or any other difficult emotion will help you move through it. Inner *work* is aptly named, you might remind yourself.

Hurrying or rushing through life's challenges, gulping them down so as to avoid pain, is not the happy or thriving place for the Seven, but the place of survival. Learning the area of avoidance and getting very familiar with it is very helpful. To this end, operating from a one-word mantra can be a powerful anecdote to the unconscious forces of "running to the light." Let's say, for example, that a Seven parent is having a painful conversation with her eleven-year-old daughter who is sharing the trials of her world. As a Seven, you want to run from that sadness to anything easier (i.e. offering her a cookie) in order to escape her pain, which may in fact be calling up your own. Using the mantra "Stay" will help the Seven learn that staying with it, staying present, and focusing is cultivating your holy work.

The Wellness Map of Type Seven, The Joyful Adventurer

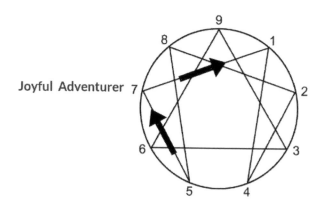

As mentioned throughout this book, each of the nine universal types on Enneagram spectrum has its own gifts and challenges. And for each personality there is what I call a Wellness Map, which shows our points of integration and disintegration with regard to emotional wellness. You can be, as a therapist once called me, "decidedly better," or not. You cannot avoid all stress in life because you are human. You can choose healthier responses instead of stressful reactions. It is *always* a choice.

The Joyful Adventurer type brings to the table a lightness of being. Maybe you have one in your family or are one yourself. Known as an optimist and the Tinkerbell of the Enneagram, the Joyful Adventurer likes to see and follow the light; this is why this type is often referred to as "free spirited." You like to enlighten, as in unburden, and perhaps your greatest gift is your immense capacity to feel gratitude.

When the Joyful Adventurer is centered and connected, you feel your joy and contentment, and you feel resourceful. You see the big picture of things and have a healthy non-attachment to outcomes. You are present. You are operating out of the bigger part of yourself when a challenge presents itself, and you choose not to run from the limits, helplessness or pain; rather, you choose to face it, stay with it and work it through.

When a Seven is centered and receiving from the high side of Five, The Wise Observer, you might tell yourself the easiest way out is through. You know if you stay with the difficulties, or feelings of helplessness, you will see your way through the challenge.

"This Too Shall Pass" is a good mantra for Sevens. With patience you ultimately get to the "big picture," and can choose to practice the healthy detachment that comes from the resourceful side of the Wise Observer. *Staying with this* limit or challenge certainly doesn't feel light, but it is practicing emotional wellness for the Joyful Adventurer.

On the other hand, when you cover up your pain, you are filling yourself up with some kind of pleasure. Remember, gluttony is a kind of "filling up" with anything that feels easier, that has more light. A filling up on pleasure, plans, and internal criticisms along with perfectionistic thinking only further contaminates the helplessness the Joyful Adventurer feels. And so the wheels spin. You are running from the limit, keeping it out of your awareness, and repressing it.

When the stress of life is unchecked, you end up in a downward spiral of not being enough. For the Joyful Adventurer, this criticism comes from the low side of Type One, The Good Reformer. Perfectionism from the Good Reformer's low side escalates your gluttony, which can be felt as a scattering, splintering type of behavior.

This is when it's time to hit the internal GPS course correct button, and say to yourself, "Don't go there."

In my Enneagram self-talk, when spiraling down with gluttony and perfectionism on overdrive, I center by telling myself, "This is not your problem!" In every situation, you get to choose your response, and with a deeper understanding of who you are, and what your patterns look like, you can replace old ineffective behaviors.

With patience, the Joyful Adventurer type gets back to the intersection of enlightened joy and healthful detachment, your "heaven on earth."

Stress is inevitable, but moment to moment it is your choice how you respond. Before my Enneagram practice, I equated happiness with rising excitement based on external circumstances. Now, being calm and centered is my deepest joy.

Whatever the challenges you find within your unique personality, your Wellness Map can help you with your healthy responses, which ultimately may have a cumulative effect on your overall health.

In summary, your Wellness Map as a Seven, The Joyful Adventurer is as follows: In times of centering and safety, you are attracting within yourself the high side of Type Five, The Wise Observer (healthful detachment, big picture, non-judgmental) and in times of tension and stress you are attracting within yourself the low side of Type One, The Good Reformer (scattering and splintering out, and a critical, righteous or perfectionistic reactivity).

This is your general behavioral pattern. Remember, *you can* access the high side and low side of all of the nine types on the spectrum.

The Instinctual Center of Type Seven, The Joyful Adventurer

The head is the dominant instinctual center for the Joyful Adventurer; these types are comfortable in their heads – be it planning, remembering dates, analyzing a current situation or problem solving. When in tension or stress they tend to over-analyze or obsess, and the monkey mind starts racing. You may not be able to fall asleep at night because you have a plethora of thoughts going round and round. Your task then, is to balance yourself by getting information and insights from your heart and gut center.

In stress a Seven may turn to obsessing and spinning their wheels, which in turn causes more anxiety. You may think, "I see all the possibilities. If I see them, I must say something or, if I missed a detail, then what?" And on and on, your mind on overdrive runs you ragged.

Anxiety is a normal emotion felt by all of us at times, and it can be a signal for a particular response. It is at the precise time of overthinking that the Joyful Adventurer needs to stop and note this overactive head center. A tired head center can imagine all kinds of scary things. If you check in with your heart and gut, and ask the same question about the issue at hand, eventually you will have answers that feel right.

For example, if you are upset about a particular person's behavior to one of your family members, and feel your mind racing about it, causing anxiety, getting aligned within your centers will help you solve your problem.

Try slowing down, putting your hands over your heart and asking, "What do I really feel here?" Dropping down into your heart space may help you get clarity about the situation. It might look like this: "Do I really have something to be afraid of here? Is this truly a mean person, one who wants to cause a lot of trouble, or just one who is in a misunderstanding and acting defensively?

Then put your hands over the low part of your belly, your gut center, and ask the same question and see what your reaction is.

When all three of these centers – head, heart and gut – harmonize in their information for you, you are in alignment, or balanced, and you will have an answer to your problem or issue that feels right.

The Wing Style of Type Seven, The Joyful Adventurer

The wing styles for The Joyful Adventurer are Type Six, The Loyal Skeptic and Type Eight, The Powerful Protector. As mentioned throughout this book, for the vast majority of people, one of these wing styles is dominant and influences the core personality type.

If you are a Joyful Adventurer with Type Six, The Loyal Skeptic as your dominant wing style, and you identify most often with the high side and gifts of the Six, the Six's vigilance might slow you down and assist you in completing tasks. In addition, both The Joyful Adventurer and The Loyal Skeptic types are gracious, charming, trusting and carefree when centered, so those qualities may be multiplied within the Joyful Adventurer type.

When problem solving, you can tell yourself that things aren't always black and white; in fact, there are often shades of gray. You can adopt both/and point of view rather than taking an either/or stance. This flexibility and the courage to just *be* may assist the Seven in your childlike responsiveness and authenticity.

If on the other hand the Seven comes from the low side of Six then the challenges of the Six can affect the Seven. At this low side of your Six wing you may a have tendency to second-guess, doubt and fear things, as well as a critical and righteous attitude. Instead of a having carefree attitude, you can get paralyzed with fear. There is a saying, "Worry is Worshipping the Problem" and that obsessing can easily happen when the Joyful Adventurer is influenced by the behavior patterns of the low side of the Loyal Skeptic. Understanding these patterns can assist in letting them go and replacing them with healthier responses.

If the you are a Joyful Adventurer who identifies with your Type Eight, The Powerful Protector wing and is operating on the high side of Eight, you will assert yourself and work for justice for all. You will be dynamic in owning your power and help others to do the same. You will have excellent leadership qualities, along with your positive nature.

If your general pattern is to identify with the low side of Eight, you will be a dominant, "in your face" type. You may not listen well, but rather speed up and be like a bull in a china shop in your interactions.

It is important to remember that the low, less resourceful side of any core personality type encompasses stress reactions built from places within us when we were surviving. New ways that feel much better than surviving are possible for each of us, no matter which type we fall within on the Enneagram.

Ways for Type Seven, The Joyful Adventurer to Practice Balance

1. Less is more for healthy Joyful Adventurers. Practice doing less, saying less, buying less, cooking and serving less. You will splinter off less, and find yourself integrated and present.

2. Say No. Work at liking limits. Work at not over-extending yourself. A full load piled high with more added on every time you splinter out will find you feeling buried. This can be tough in a culture that rewards exhaustion, but with your deepened awareness you can and will take on "just enough."

3. Remember and practice this mantra: "Focus is my w-holy work." Let your bowl of life get half-emptied before you refill it with over-planning. Feel what "less is more" feels like and give yourself a chance to enjoy it.

4. Realize that you bring gratitude to the table, which is one of the highest expressions of joy we have in this life. One way to continue cultivating this wonderful aspect within you is to say, as "Infinite love and gratitude" to small and great things. That mantra can put things in perspective.

5. When tension rises and distraction sets in, remind yourself, "The more hurried I go the behind-er I get." Say, "I can set limits for myself without feeling deprived."

6. STAY. Observe in yourself what I call "Tinkerbellitis," a perpetual chasing of the light and running from any darkness or pain, instead of working through the painful

limit.

7. Be an active listener. Let others have the spotlight on their field of interest, or topic of the hour. Show them you are listening with your facial expressions.

8. When things feel too limiting or painful slow down the anxiety train by remembering, "This too shall pass."

9. Breath work is good for centering. It is an inspiring practice when tension rises and you are not sure what to do. Here is an effective breath work exercise: inhale to a count of seven, then hold to a count of four, and exhale to a count of seven. This necessary yet simple breath work will positively affect anything you are facing or racing toward.

10. Cultivate quiet spaces and meditation. In time and with practice you will crave healthful presence in the same way you used to crave stimulation.

CHAPTER EIGHT

Type Eight,
The Powerful Protector

"In your vulnerability you will find strength."

A Short Story of a Powerful Protector

On a recent flight I was sitting two rows behind the exit row. A few minutes after takeoff, the flight attendant stood by that row and started the usual talk about the responsibilities of those passengers should there be a problem during the flight. She asked them for their attention, however, as she began asking some routine questions she noticed that a young female passenger on the end of the row was not looking up.

With the expression of a very frustrated parent who feels ignored as they state rules to their teen, the flight attendant said,

"If you do not want to take this responsibility in the exit row seriously, then we can move you."

The woman looked up and said, "No, I was paying attention."

The flight attendant resumed her speech, but almost immediately I was startled by a stern voice stating, "THAT'S IT, you are moving – you need to pay attention to what I am saying and you clearly do not take this seriously."

When the young lady objected and argued, the flight attendant said, "You have a choice to move to Seat 29 immediately or you will be escorted off the plane."

Several of us looked around with a look of *WHAT?!* on our faces. Although this young lady clearly didn't get the sense of urgency of the situation, the flight attendant's disciplinary action seemed harsh. The tension was so thick you could cut it with a knife.

It seemed to me that she might not have talked to an older person like that. Then again, maybe an older person would have listened to her with more active attention. My immediate hunch was this flight attendant was having a bad afternoon, was stressed and was ramping up her relative position of power on an airplane.

Many of us turned to each other with a look of, "Yikes, what's going to happen next?"

After finishing her routine, the flight attendant sat down in her seat facing the exit row and quietly said to some passengers, "I am not going to take that kind of behavior." Then she switched gears and went into a pleasant conversation mode. Some passengers acquiesced or agreed and some said nothing.

Many of my clients with a Type Eight, The Powerful Protector core personality, upon careful reflection, admit that when they are stressed, their go-to behavior is the sort of domineering display seen in the flight attendant.

Perhaps in a better moment, she might have softened her tone and used diplomacy, saying something like, "I really need everyone in the exit rows to look up and show me that they hear me. It may seem routine and unimportant, but our airline is very serious about your responsibility in this row."

Instead, she clearly got upset by the perceived lack of respect this passenger was showing her; however, just because the young woman was looking down doesn't mean she wasn't listening. The attendant was almost on top of them and it was pretty obvious they could hear her. The Flight attendant certainly deserved respect and attention and in an ideal world, all eyes would be upon her. However, due to the frequency of these routine speeches, people can look like they are not paying attention.

The Flight attendant's supervisor would most likely have said of this situation, "Finding diplomatic ways to highlight the safety rules without confronting the passenger is important."

Threatening to escort someone off the plane because they didn't look at you the moment you began speaking is not using diplomacy.

When The Powerful Protector types barge into situations with a "put up your dukes," attitude, instead of expecting a meeting of the minds, you can bet they are stressed.

If you are a centered Powerful Protector type, there is an interdependence present, an equanimity, instead of a Little Red

Hen attitude of over-independence. When centered and secure, Powerful Protector types are quite disarming and giving. They believe that most people would never intentionally hurt anyone and know people are good at heart or have the potential to be so. They give the benefit of the doubt, with an inherent trust in the other. When you share yourself in a way that some people would say seems larger than life, you own your power and you want to help the rest of us own ours.

The Strengths and Challenges of Type Eight, The Powerful Protector

Strengths The Power Protector brings to the table:

Owns power

Assertion

Clear communication

Energetic

Enthusiastic (God is with us)

Dynamic

Charismatic

Present

Innocence

Wants justice

Underdog protector

Honest

Challenges The Powerful Protector brings to the table:

Domineering

Controlling

Out of touch with the feminine, receptive side

Confronting

Charging after

Over the top

Nosy

Bossy

My way or the highway

Aggressive

Anger management

Bull in a china shop

The Emotional Passion of Type Eight, The Powerful Protector

The emotional passion of The Powerful Protector is lust. Your first thought when you read the word "lust" was that it is about strong sexual desire. While the Type Eight's emotional passion could include sexual desire, in this context it is more about a general excess or desire for control.

Again, remember that lust itself is neither right nor wrong. Certainly when we hear a lyric from Camelot about "the lusty month of May," we think positive things. We get the sexual undertone but we may also think of the beauty of the green floral growth in May. Lusty Spring is growth popping up all over.

Lust or excess in life is not always a problem. I have a therapist friend who has a pillow on her couch that says, "Too much of a Good Thing is Wonderful." (Author unknown)

Another friend has another anonymous lusty quote under her email signature: "Excess on occasion is exhilarating. It prevents moderation from acquiring the deadening effect of habit."

So many of us have been taught to be quiet, to be careful, to be small, to be humble. Lust or excess can balance boredom, and yet balance is the operative word here. To be managed by lust is to be managed by excess, or an excessive need for control, and that kind of energy can be difficult to be around.

Perspective is important here – one person's excess is another person's boredom. It is your life canvas to create and live from in a healthful way. It is in this balance that you find your emotional health. When Powerful Protectors share with, not dominate, the other, they are giving and even assist the underdog. Eights who do not manage lust, are often me-firsters, loud, aggressive, confronting and in a word, overbearing. At the unhealthiest levels they act without boundaries, destructive, even terrorizing others.

When a Powerful Protector is managing or directing your emotional passion of lust or control you are able to temper yourself. You can hold back, be last, and self-surrender. You can use your desire for control positively, to control yourself. This quote from Dr. Darren Weissman is especially apropos: "When you cannot control what is happening, challenge yourself to control the way you respond to what is happening. That's where your power is."

Mastering your emotional passions is a lifelong process, whichever your type. It is so worth this inner work, if you are looking to own your power.

Powerful Protectors at the high end, when centered are identifying and managing your emotional passion of lust. It is here you are attracting within the high side of Type Two, The Loving Giver.

You are resourceful, assertive, active and magnanimous. Your giving merges with your deepened awareness. You care how you are affecting others. You slow down the driving energy of excessive control. This practice enriches your life and the life of others. You may let go and encourage another to lead.

A symbol for Type Eight is fire. Fire is a powerful force. A contained fire can warm your home, and nourish your body with a good meal. An uncontained fire can do harm. At the high side, and when Powerful Protectors use self-restraint consciously, they are containing or managing their fire. When this happens, they practice self-mastery.

The Area of Avoidance for Type Eight, The Powerful Protector

The area of avoidance or blind spot for The Powerful Protector is weakness or vulnerability.

It has likely developed around a combination of forces, including your desire to be the strongest or dominant force in a group. This may be because others dominated you when you were growing up or you may have witnessed considerable power struggles in your family.

You have worked hard at being strong, so at a glance, any weakness and vulnerability seem to be the opposite of strength. You learned to go against the grain and push against "the forces that be" as a way to survive.

You are learning that vulnerability can indeed be, not the opposite of strength, but the core of it.

My friend has a coffee mug which says, *Vulnerability is the New Strong*. To be in touch and in tune with your vulnerability is true strength. When you are authentic and connected to your feelings, you can better access what is true for you.

When a Powerful Protector is in a trouble spot in life, avoiding your vulnerability is often an indicator that you are out of touch with the connection between strong and vulnerable. You are stuck in "old tapes" that state being vulnerable means being weak and that is not a good thing. You stay in positions of false power, using intimidation or confrontation to manipulate others.

When you are stressed and feeling confrontational, avoiding feeling your own vulnerability, or unaware of this pattern, your shadow side is leading you. Because you may be blind to this self-knowledge, the area of avoidance is a blind spot.

When an Eight is in these unhealthy patterns of thinking and feeling, an assertive person might call them out on their bully behavior, or people may acquiesce and cower. When you realize the effect that avoiding your vulnerability has on other people, you are on the right path. With this awareness practice you will know that when you are acting with intimidation or dominance, things will feel out of balance.

You will want more interdependence and less independence. Your "I will do it myself" mentality may subside. An interest in dominating will not have appeal for the Eight when you are safe and secure. You will want equanimity and fairness for all, even consulting the underdog.

Your larger-than-life persona may tone down for the good of the group. You will remain assertive but not aggressive. You will have more humility and ask more questions, rather than giving declarative answers. You may remind yourself that you don't have all of the answers and feel freer because of it. Your active masculine side will find your receptive feminine side and therein you will find your balance.

The Wellness Map for Type Eight, the Powerful Protector

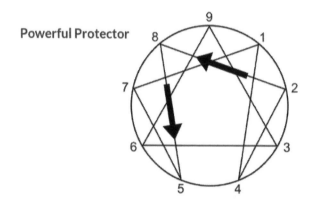

Powerful Protector

When Powerful Protector types are centered, you attract within or receive from the high aspects of personality Type Two, The Loving Giver. You own your power and help others do the same.

On the other hand, when feeling stressed or insecure you attract within or receive from the lower aspects of Type Five, The Wise Observer. This is where you isolate into that real or metaphorical cave – that one in your head.

When you as The Powerful Protector feel secure, you live from the resourceful or high side of yourself. You tap into your resources. You co-create with Source, You *Re-source!* This is of course true whatever your personality type. For the Eight, this means you are your own person, acting assertively, not aggressively. It also means you are highly considerate, and protective of others, especially the underdog.

In times of security, when you feel centered, you are clear, caring, and action-oriented. You like to take the lead on a challenging project and you meet it head-on with great enthusiasm. You may have a partner or team that you guide, protect and provide great leadership for, and encourage them to contribute. You are magnanimous without needing to dominate.

Much like the way of resourceful Type Three, The Effective Achiever, you use your energy to get the job done in a cooperative, not controlling, way. Here you are in touch with your honorable, hard-working self who is competent *and* compassionate. You can manage the ego's need to dominate or overwhelm others. You let down your guard for the sake of all involved.

If you are feeling stressed or insecure, you attract within, or receive from, the lower aspects of Type Five, The Wise Observer. This is the place of withholding yourself because you are afraid of or uncomfortable with your feelings. If you are not comfortable with your own feelings, it is safe to say that you are not comfortable with others sharing their feelings, so you retreat.

Other people can be in the room when you are isolating yourself and so, you become withholding, distant, stand-offish, or even cold.

Sometimes even the mere presence others can feel off-putting if a Powerful Protector is stressed, and so you too can retreat into a more tangible space, such as a man cave or she shed, or you may feel angry and resentful, with a "who needs them anyway" attitude.

When stressed, you can be overwhelming for people because you seem dominating and overly forceful to them. They even find that kind of energy distasteful and go away from you. This may create tension between you and those closest to you.

When you are aware of your imbalance in your masculine and feminine sides, and your masculine side is on overdrive, being intimidating, insensitive, and bully-ish, you know it is time to use this Wellness Map and do an inner course correction.

Once you are more centered you start receiving or attracting again from the high side of The Loving Giver. Receiving the other and their ideas will bring forth compassion and protection for the other. This is a much more fulfilling and happy place for the Eight to be, although the ego would fool you into thinking otherwise.

Going habitual is very easy, and can actually feel very comfortable initially. It is a common thing for all of us to do. Being on automatic, losing your self-mastery and/or being ego-driven instead of center-driven may be your habitual place. *However, that is not truly your happy place, not your place of well-being.*

In your authentic, essential self lies your well-being and true happiness. With practice you can get to this desired state, where you are aware of your passion but not mastered by it. You are not in denial or interested in being in denial. You are interested in and therefore invested in being conscious, safe, secure, centered, graced and in process.

Plato's quote may be worth reflection here, "An unexamined life is not worth living."

In summary, your Wellness Map for Type 8, The Powerful Protector is as follows: In times of centering and safety, you are attracting within yourself the high side of Type Two, The Loving Giver (service and justice for all) and in times of tension and stress you are attracting within yourself the low side of Type Five, The Wise Observer (control, isolation and withholding) This is your general behavioral pattern. Remember, *you can* access the high side and low side of all of the nine types on the spectrum.

The Instinctual Center of Type Eight, The Powerful Protector

The gut or body is the dominant instinctual center for the Type Eight, The Protector. Wisdom comes in the form of a gut feeling and this is your preferred way of knowing something.

You are very clear when you are centered and secure. Your clarity and your ability to be assertive is derived from the knowing in your gut.

The "no B.S." way you like to be with people and your

ability to let down your guard and be disarming shows you believe in equanimity. And, as cliché as it may sound, when Powerful Protectors remember and practice that "there is no I in team," they are on the track to center. A team or partner mentality can help to subdue the Eight's lust or need to have a hand in everything.

When you use your assertive skills to fight on behalf of the underdog, your heart center is activated. When you slow down the train of your reactivity, and think something through as well as react to the feeling/sensation in your gut, you may calm yourself down. When you trust your heart and mind over these gut reactions, you find you have thoughtful and compassionate responses, not just reactions. This process of engaging the heart and the mind with the gut is to feel aligned in body (gut) mind (head) and spirit (heart).

When tension starts to rise and you are feeling stressed, you may feel a compulsive need to control every little thing. On automatic, when you go into this stressful place, you feel vulnerable and don't like it, so you can cover it up with a macho kind of behavior.

In this reactive state, your gut center is on overdrive; it is dangerous to problem solve from here. It is helpful to get in touch with the vulnerability you are avoiding. A powerful way to slow down the reactivity is to check in, that is, pose the question or problem at hand to all three centers. Aligning the instinctual centers when problem solving is a process and can take a few minutes or a few days. It is like putting a puzzle together. Sometimes it comes together easily and sometimes it takes patience. However, only when they are in agreement should you move on the problem.

The goal is to solve the problem not from a place of gut reactivity or heart drama or monkey mind, but to use the body wisdom, along with the bright mind and the heart's compassion, to get to our truth in the matter.

We make choices all day long. How many do we make from this wonderful place of alignment within the three centers? Again, it is healthy for Powerful Protectors to repeat and remember, "Balance of my centers is the key to my true power."

The Wing Style of Type Eight, The Powerful Protector

Type Eight, The Powerful Protector has as its wing styles Type Seven, The Joyful Adventurer and Type Nine, The Peaceful Mediator. If The Joyful Adventurer is your dominant wing and you generally identify with the high side of that wing, your Powerful Protector style may be able to embrace being vulnerable. You may be willing to laugh at yourself and tell on yourself. You may like to lighten up.

You will see the big picture more often, meaning you realize that you see only a glimpse of it, just as we all do, considering that at this point in our evolution most of us use only ten percent of our brain capacity. You don't take yourself too seriously if you identify with the high side of Seven. You lead not by being "the heavy" but with humor and a sense of genuine teamwork, and an attitude of "many hands make light work."

If you identify generally with the low side of your Seven wing you may scatter or splinter away your power. You may have potential to lead but feel overwhelmed. You may not have the staying power it takes to lead others effectively.

If your Type Nine, Peaceful Mediator wing is dominant, and if you identify with its higher side, this may help subdue your Powerful Protector personality, and may for example hold you back from excess. You may mediate more than dominate. You might be very effective at leading with a harmony-in-action mantra.

On the other hand, if you identify with the lower side of Nine, your Peaceful Mediator wing may affect your personality in ways of self-forgetting. Your need for excess may get masked as "whatever." You may not be aggressive or dominant but rather passive-aggressive and manipulative in your expression. You may dial down and withdraw or withhold more if things get tense or stressed.

Ways for Type Eight, The Powerful Protector to Practice Balance

1. Continue to own your power, and teach others how to be empowered as well.

2. Resist the urge to dominate situations. Look for fairness, balance and equanimity.

3. Be last, be passive, be quieter. People will appreciate you for this effort.

4. When tension rises, and your intensity is ramping up, breathe into it instead.

5. When you are resisting the urge to control and dominate others, you release your fear that they will dominate you.

6. Keep your belief that we are all born in innocence and so why would we want to hurt each other? This good will empowers all.

7. Let your guard down; allow others to give their affection and attention to you, especially when you feel you do not need anyone.

8. Practice fair play and justice for all. Avoid arrogance and judgment of others. All people have something to offer.

9. When you feel the anger or "fight" rising up in you, own it, and be aware of your body's cues.

10. Pay attention to when you are becoming reclusive. This is a clue to your need for space and time to identify your feelings, which will always help the situation.

CHAPTER NINE

Type Nine, The Peaceful Mediator

"Resolve little things before they become big things, like health issues."

A Short Story of a Peaceful Mediator

As someone who was raised by a Peaceful Mediator (my mother) and married to one for thirty-seven years, I know this type well, very well.

When I completed my first Master's level certification within the Enneagram, I was very excited about it. I was also excited to share it with my husband. We had led Discovery Weekend retreats for Engaged couples patterned after Marriage Encounter, so we had certainly gotten into deep discussions about our own personalities.

When we talked about my husband being The Peaceful Type on the Enneagram, he said, "What is so bad about being peaceful, seeing all sides, and merging with others, not speaking up? It feels okay to me."

Of course I reminded him that we are all in this together, that we all have sunny and shadow sides and have inner work to do for personal growth.

"We are not just picking on the peaceful types here," I explained. I then asked him, "Remember how you said to me when we first fell in love, that you didn't think you had ever been or would ever be really happy? Do you think that by merging with others too much and not really hearing your own voice you feel in a way like you never really are heard and that this alone can affect your happiness?"

I continued, careful not to be the therapist but a loving partner, "Do you see that as being a peacemaker sometimes you abandon yourself? Everyone likes to be heard, maybe not in the same vocal way but somehow they need to express themselves, and if they are not, I'm guessing that doesn't feel good or *happy*.

I continued, "You know how to express yourself even when you feel tense and worried about conflict, but deep down, I believe you would like to express yourself more often, even if you tell people differently. When you answer with 'whatever,' and are not willing to say what you mean and mean what you say, I think that makes you feel somewhat unhappy. Does that make sense to you?"

"Oh, and as a Peaceful Mediator parent, disciplining kids

140

can feel uncomfortable because you want to run from the conflict. When you run, I get to be the 'bad cop.' So, there is also *that.*"

"Oh yeah," he said as the light went on inside.

In every Enneagram type there is a tendency and a task. There is a paradox in each one. As a peacemaker type, the peace process holds tension and even conflict along the way. If you self-forget to a fault, and are not heard, over time, as a peaceful type, you simply get numb or choose to numb out feelings through some other form of distraction. Answering people with "whatever" from this place is not true peace or happiness for the many clients or students I have that fall within that type.

I'm happy to say the love of my life, my husband, has received a lot of insight from learning that a healthy Peaceful Mediator Type's kind of heaven on earth is when he experiences harmony and love *in action*, and a big component of that happiness is being heard and resolving little things before they become big things.

The Strengths and Challenges of Type Nine, The Peaceful Mediator

Strengths that the Peaceful Mediator brings to the table:

Calming presence

Attention to nuance

Wind beneath our wings

Kindness

Mediating/seeing both sides

Good compromiser

Harmonizer

Love in action

Low expectations

Can "let it go"

Challenges that The Peaceful Mediator brings to the table:

Has trouble discriminating wants and needs, indecisive

Self-forgetting

Passive-aggressive

Manipulative

Wants to fix, not feel

Withholding

Over-pleaser

Inattentive

Runs from conflict,

Doesn't resolve little things which can turn into big things

The Emotional Passion of Type Nine, The Peaceful Mediator

The Emotional Passion of the Nine is sloth. I remembered reading this on my husband's completed Enneagram profile and thinking, sloth means lazy, right? He is the farthest thing from lazy. Of course, deepening awareness asks us to look carefully, dig more deeply.

This was not about my husband's ability to get a zillion things done in a day. Sloth in this context means a laziness of self; of self-expression, of being heard, or a kind of self-forgetting, especially in tension or conflict. A form of withdrawing or shutting down.

After careful reflection about my husband's patterns when stressed, I thoughtfully said to myself, "Oh. That. Yes. I see."

Remember that emotional passions are not right or wrong. I reiterate this in every chapter because my students continue to ask when I teach about them things like "That is the down side of my type, right?" And I say, "Passions, they just are. It is how we face and work through them – or manage them – that matters."

The sloth is a slow-moving animal. They are beautiful in their turtle-like motions and it can actually be very relaxing to watch them in their *nice and easy does it* kind of way.

To be slothful or lazy gets such a bad rap in a "chipmunks on roller skates" culture. Slowing down is what allows a Nine to pay attention to nuance. Slowing down is what makes you vigilant. Slowing down helps a Peaceful Type hear your truth and intuition within so you can be effective. Slowing down the train and taking breaths to see shades of grey is calming to all of us. It is when the emotional passion of sloth or laziness of self-expression becomes unaware, unmanaged, self-forgetting that it can become a hindrance rather than a help to a Peaceful Mediator.

Everyone wants to be heard. Even Peaceful Mediators, who say they don't need or want to express themselves, do have this need; they just may want to do it in their own way.

When my husband expressed himself to our teenagers about anger and tempers and set a firm boundary about basic respect, specifically language, that reflected that respect in our household, he felt good about himself.

However, when he ignored this basic fatherly responsibility, of co-discipline for a disrespectful fighting teenager, he forgot himself, and his essential expression of being love and harmony in action.

When Peaceful Mediators avoid the conflicts and resolution of those conflicts and get habitual about withdrawing, they do not feel good about themselves. Self-forgetting or dialing down to a fault is not a virtue. It is not being peaceful or calm. It is hiding, merging too much in the shades of grey, and is essentially a cop-out. It is what happens to a Peaceful Mediator when your emotional passion of sloth or self-forgetting is running you all over town with a ring in your nose. Remember we are all in this together.

When this emotional passion is your master, you are in some form of stress or unawareness. When you name and work your passion through, you feel your self- discipline and mastery growing.

Naming the tendency to be slothful or lazy when it comes to your own expression is always the first step to reconnecting with your deepened awareness, which is in a big part, managing the emotional passion.

An exercise for self-awareness that we do in my workshops is saying thank you to our passions; for example, "Thank you, Emotional Passion. There are good things that come from you within me, but I lead the dance here. "

If you are a Peaceful Mediator, your self-talk might go this way: "Thank you, emotional passion of sloth or self-forgetting. Because of you, so long as I am directing you, I can be humble, contained, and vigilant. The thing is, I do *like* to be heard – to express myself – even if I fool myself into thinking I don't. It's a great feeling to express in my own unique way."

The Thank you exercise is a healthy practice for any of the Enneagram Types in the self-mastery process.

The Area of Avoidance of Type Nine, The Peaceful Mediator

The area of avoidance for the Peaceful Mediator is conflict. Conflict has different shades, and includes mild tension all the way to violence; think pale pink to blood red.

When you think about conflict, whatever your personality type, if you are feeling passive not aggressive, you may feel a tendency to avoid tension or conflict. You might be thinking, "Well, who wants conflict?"; however, for a Type Nine, this knee-jerk reaction may be an indicator that you are avoiding in an unhealthy way.

Conflict needs to be unpacked here. Problems and conflicts are all around and within us. It is not conflict that is inherently negative, but the absence of resolutions of conflict that is sad.

I remember having a phone conversation with my young daughter's friend's mom. It was about a minor fourth grade scuffle.

I said to the mom, who I considered a friend as well, "I am

sure we can resolve the problem."

"There's nothing to resolve," she coldly replied, then never again spoke to my ten-year-old daughter, even after she sent a letter of apology for her part in the kid's fight. In not letting our kids play together, this mom was clearly resolving the situation in a passive aggressive manner.

When Peaceful Mediators are centered they act from a desire for harmony in action. A stressed Peaceful Mediator, however, can have patterns of passive-aggressive behavior. This person could have gone through the "front door" directly and been heard, and listened to our side of the story too, and we could have come to a resolution.

She chose instead to go through the "back door," saying there was no problem, nothing to resolve, being manipulative in her actions. This was not harmony in action. The conflict and lack of resolution around it seemed to show the other mom's fear and cowardice.

Peaceful personality types developed in part because they waited for things to resolve themselves, moved away from others, and dialed down their own feelings, because this helped them to survive not being heard.

If your tendency is to dial down withdrawing from conflict, then your task for balance is to learn how to resolve it. Resolving little things before they become big things is the healthy Peaceful Mediator's primary task. When in a trouble spot, naming this area of avoidance or blind spot is often the start of the conflict resolution process.

On the other hand, avoiding or denying things your spirit wants you to face and own always has consequences. There was a line I loved in *The Martian,* a movie about an astronaut played by Matt Damon who found himself alone on Mars. He was feeling stressed with challenge after challenge on the planet. He centered himself with an inner knowing and said, and I am paraphrasing, "Life is just about problem-solving." This is a healthy mantra for all of us, and especially The Peaceful Mediator, who often needs to remind themselves that the *easiest way out is through.*

Working through problems and conflicts, being present to your resolution work, is what makes you feel truly effective.

The Wellness Map of Type Nine, The Peaceful Mediator

Peaceful Mediator

When The Peaceful Mediator centers and connects within, you receive from the high side of Type Three, The Effective Achiever. When you are stressed or disconnected from yourself, you receive or attract within, the low aspects of Type Six, The Loyal Skeptic.

The higher aspects of Type Three, The Effective Achiever include being motivated to action by your inner truth, being goal-oriented, and successful. For Peaceful Mediators, putting love and harmony in action is your heaven on earth, your deeply happy place. The gifts of the Peaceful Mediator and The Effective Achiever are a powerful combination. It is also your trajectory for your well-being in life.

When centered, you are peaceful and calm but not to a fault. You are willing to go against the grain and assert your view, even if it is not the most popular opinion at the table. You are motivated by your inner truths and are willing to be heard even if it might ruffle some feathers. You are gaining comfort naming your tendency to self-forget and merge with others. You may concern yourself less with a "peace at any price," attitude and be more willing to share your feelings.

With stress and disconnection, all of the nine universal personality types domino down and attract the low side of another type. The Peaceful Mediator in stress attracts within or receives the low aspects of Type Six, the Loyal Skeptic. As mentioned earlier, the low side of The Peaceful Mediator includes self-forgetting and merging too much with others. When this behavior gets contaminated with the low side of Type Six, The Loyal Skeptic, The Peaceful Mediator can then turn to second guessing and being over-vigilant, a "doubting Thomas." The Six's fear can also show up as irritation or anger; remember the scared dog that bites.

It is in these states, when you are unaware that you are slothful in your self-expression, you may appear mellow, saying, "Whatever," or "What's the big deal if I don't express myself?"

Not speaking up for yourself because it doesn't feel important enough (i.e. YOU don't feel important enough) to make waves, upon reflection, can make you feel disappointed in yourself.

Your shrinking around others, so you don't upset them with your real feelings and ideas, contributes to the unkind label of doormat or milk toast for the low side of Peaceful Mediator.

When you get an insight, however subtle it may be, that you are abandoning yourself in your relationships, you are on the path to self-expression and being heard.

Your thinking and feeling may get acted out in low side of Loyal Skeptic, behavior which includes resisting authority, or clinging to it defensively. This is not your happy place, no matter how habitually comfortable it seems. You may go in and out of these high and low sides of your personality type, as we all do to one degree or another. As you deepen your awareness and see your new and healthier actions causing shifts in your life for the better, you can navigate through these low sides. You can get back to the thriving higher side, or your "heaven on earth."

"The gold is in the dark," said Carl Jung, and when The Peaceful Mediator wakes up to their style of being overly dialed-down communicators who self-forget *and* second guess to a fault, you can see this is not where you feel truly well. You can begin your inner GPS course correction back to feeling well. This is where you are centered, safe and secure and you are being effective agents of harmony in action.

As you turn on your inner GPS, you see conflicts that can be resolved, and waves that can be settled. You feel more of your love and harmony in action, and *in action* implies being *heard*, not forgetting yourself.

In summary, the Wellness Map for The Peaceful Mediator is as follows: In times of centering and safety, you are attracting within yourself the high side of Type Three, The Effective Achiever, and in times of tension and stress you are attracting within yourself the low side of Type Six, The Loyal Skeptic.

This is your general behavioral pattern. Remember *you can* access the high side and low side of all of the nine types on the spectrum.

The Instinctual Center of Type Nine, The Peaceful Mediator

The dominant instinctual center of the Peaceful Mediator is the gut. Your bellyful of information speaks loudly to you and is loaded with insight when you are feeling safe and secure. When you are centered, as a Nine, you can sense your deepest truth in your gut and be motivated to act upon it.

When you are stressed, however, you can go from a usual disconnected and unresponsive note to a fast and furious one. The knee-jerk reaction comes out of the blue if you've been squelching your anger for too long.

When you are in stress, the doubt and fear in your gut can numb you out. You might gray everything, and think "What's the difference?"

When you are stressed, you may act aggressively. If your fear manifests as a counter-phobic state, it can feel to others as if you are trying to control them. You can swing from passive aggressive to acting aggressive in the form of micro-managing, or even exploding at someone.

Again, this is usually after you've held your thoughts and feelings in for too long or denied your self-expression.

If someone says to you, after you've exploded at them, "Where did that come from?" it is healthy to say, "I don't always feel heard. I'm trying to express myself more often and at times it is difficult for me."

Change begins with the first step and no one ever said the first steps are easy. Feel good about the fact that you are making them, even if it seems like the hundredth time. That is how it can feel for all of us, and you will see progress if you keep working at asserting yourself. One of the reasons that Nines like action is because it is a vehicle for your self-expression. Action just speaks louder to you than words. Remember, however, that words can be effective too.

In stress, the information from your overactive gut center is alerting you to a self that feels insecure, or off center. Becoming familiar with what you look and feel like when you are disconnected will help you back to center.

When you realize you are feeling stressed you may think, "If I say this, I'll ruffle her feathers so I better not say anything." Remember that self-forgetting, or your lack of self-expression gets contaminated by your second-guessing. If you recognize this as a self -defeating pattern, you may be able to catch yourself from acting out this way. Strive to allow yourself to be heard and do your conflict resolution work in a way that makes you feel effective. This can include finding a creative way to be heard, such as journaling, or writing a letter.

For a Nine, aligning the head and heart *with* the overactive gut center can reduce the amount of times you go on auto pilot, withdraw, and second-guess. Aligning the three instinctual centers will return you to your clarity and calm. Then you will come from a deep knowing that is unshakable and motivates you to your best action.

The Wing Style of Type Nine, The Peaceful Mediator

The wing styles of the Peaceful Mediator are Type Eight, The Powerful Protector and Type One, The Good Reformer.

If Eight is your dominant wing, and you identify with the high side of this wing style then you may express yourself more often. You may be able to show justice for all, including yourself. You may let yourself be heard more even if it upsets someone. You may not worry so much about conflicts or problems because you know that conflict resolution will bring you back to fairness, which causes you to feel peaceful.

If you identify with the low side of Eight, however, you may aggressively withdraw from others and or you may alternately get controlling and bossy. You may find yourself in a lonely at the top place if you lead with a micro-managing or controlling style.

If Type One, The Good Reformer is your dominant wing and you identify with the high side of this wing style, then you will be very concerned with integrity. You will value your integrity over a "peace at any price" attitude. You may be willing to fight fair or fight for what you believe in.

Identifying with the high side of your Good Reformer wing may help you with your conflict resolution ability. You might not always feel peaceful but that will be okay with you as long as the outcome is for the higher good and may ultimately bring peace.

If you identify with the low side of One, your perfectionism may make your Peaceful Mediator personality withdraw even more from conflict because you will be second-guessing what you should or shouldn't say or do. You may attempt conflict resolution and it may not go well and so you might be hard on yourself. You might think, "I said too much again" and berate yourself to think before you speak next time. Your black and white thinking may cause you to judge others and make it impossible for them to live up to your standards.

It is important to note that on occasion an individual will identify with both wings. When this happens, it may be that you are equal parts both of your wing styles. Discerning the aspects of both Wings will be helpful in seeing how they affect your core personality.

Ways For Type Nine, The Peaceful Mediator to Practice Balance

1. Consider that in order to be happy you will need to be heard. Hiding behind a mask of, "I don't really care," is not true peace.

2. Be aware that you have a tendency to procrastinate. Doing it now will give you a sense of efficiency and energy.

3. Resist the urge to settle for too little or resign yourself too quickly. Often that is a substitute for feeling peaceful.

4. Choose a side more often. Be decisive and take a stand even if you have a nagging voice that says, "Don't rock the boat."

5. When you find yourself saying "What's the difference?" give yourself a chance to explore what the different outcomes could actually be.

6. Resist the grey areas. When you center you are really good at hearing your preferences.

7. Resolve what appear to be inconsequential things before they become big things.

8. When you want to go to your invisible place see it as a sign of your depletion. Be proactive. Ask for space or whatever it is you need before you get to this point.

9. Practice being first to ask for what you want instead of merging too much with other's desires.

10. Move more. By exercising you are expressing yourself and making yourself come alive. You will feel healthier and more effective generating your own energy.

CHAPTER TEN

The Enneagram Effect

T he Enneagram can teach you about both your human nature and divine potential. You have read a short story of each of the nine universal types; you have learned about the strengths and challenges, passions and blind spots, Wellness Maps and wing styles, instinctual centers and ways to practice balance. Remember that these mainstays are about general patterns of thinking and behaving. There may be as many nuances within each of the nine universal personality types as there are people in the world. Discovering your unique nuances is your wonderful work within the Enneagram. Your inner work is a great investment in you, and your relationships whatever combination of personal growth tools you use.

You now know that having an understanding of your personality type and your own potential is the *start* of the inner work of personal transformation. After all, actually *realizing* who you are meant to be takes more than the knowing.

Your deepened awareness and acceptance of that newfound awareness may provide a new pathway within you. Your practice of new behaviors that free you and get you out of your own way will provide you with profound shifts.

The effects you feel will be so worth any work you have done to realize your growth. Be patient with yourself. Sometimes after an aha insight, you change behavior immediately. More often, other times it takes baby steps to see progress within yourself.

The good news is that the Enneagram gives you practical ways to gain consciousness and make a resourceful choice. You will come from your own internal safety not your own often self-created stress. One way that cannot be emphasized enough is through breath work. Breathing into the emotional passion that gets triggered can help to deepen your awareness of it.

Science has now shown us that with repeated practice, we can break out of our habitual patterns and reactions more often.

Dr. Donald Hebb of McGill University has investigated the neural circuits in the brain, the connections that fire or light up when we are thinking certain thoughts or are engaged in certain behaviors. His conclusion? "What fires together wires together."

In other words, when your neural circuits fire together in a certain way repeatedly, they tend to do more of the same. In Enneagram terms, your habitual patterns make deep grooves within your personality. When you change the pattern through conscious choice, instead of continually going on autopilot, you disrupt the pattern, and the grooves, lose their edge and soften.

Liz Tobin, Family Health Practitioner, taught it to me this way:

"Connect to your detached observer within and notice how your feelings, perceptions and interactions change. The next time you are faced with a situation that pushes your buttons, stop and pause. Say to yourself, "Here is an opportunity for me to change this way of mine. I have the power to change my response. I do not have to react in the same old way.""

People can change and grow. It takes effort but like anything that gets practiced it gets easier with time.

Remember Dr. David Daniel's 4 A's related to the Enneagram: Awareness, Acceptance, Action and Adherence.

- *Awareness* of yourself is your type's wisdom that resonates within you.

- *Acceptance of* your whole self entails both sun and shadow sides.

- *Action:* making changes in your patterns by using this newfound awareness to make choices that are balanced for your greater well-being.

- *Adherence* or practice: repeatedly using your Wellness Map and Enneagram wisdom.

Becoming aware is the first step, *accepting* your new *awareness* and using strategies to create new behavior, is *action.* Repeating these new behaviors is *adherence* or practice.

With practice you will feel a shift for the better within yourself.

To maximize the Enneagram wisdom and its potential for you, I highly recommend working with a coach. Doing your inner work with a guide will provide objective feedback and support for you. Support is important when you make significant changes in life.

If you choose to self-study, it would be very helpful for you to have a journal. In your personal observations, you might write your desires for the changes you would like to see within yourself, and then write how you are doing with your new awareness and action steps. Refer back to the chapter on your type as a springboard.

I'll never forget the day my father remarked, "We grow in spite of ourselves." It was a simple but profound and philo-sophical statement. Because I was feeling that the therapy that I was in at the time was so helpful and fruitful, I replied, "Yes, Dad, but can you imagine what it looks like for you when you do the inner work?"

My father was from a generation of men who were not encouraged to work through feelings, or reflect on personality. However, he was a heart-centered guy, and at age eighty-seven he asked me "Could you bring up that psychological test you give to your clients?" I gave him a full written Enneagram reading and consult. It was wonderful to see the light go on in his eyes as the Enneagram wisdom resonated deeply within him.

This experience with my dad reminded me of a line from a Bonnie Raitt song: "Life gets mighty precious when there's less of it to waste."

He shared with me that he thought the Enneagram was a powerful tool for growth, and thanked me. He wondered what it would have been like to learn about himself at this deeper level earlier in his life.

The Enneagram Effect will be as powerful for you as the energy you put into it. I hope I have contributed to your self –

awareness, self-love and compassion for others. Keep on going deeper with this work if you are guided. You will be happy you did.

I am continually grateful for the Enneagram teachers and students who make their emotional wellness a priority and who are more often thriving because of their Enneagram wisdom and practice. Infinite love and gratitude for the deep effect that the Enneagram has had in my life, and the profound effects I have been honored to witness in the lives of others.

APPENDIX A

Enneagram Type Discernment Quiz

Which of the following 9 summaries best describes you? If you are new to the Enneagram, this quiz can help you discern your type. Read the nine summary paragraphs of each of the nine personality types on the Enneagram. Choose one type that generally feels most like you. Do not overthink it. Remember you are looking for patterns and habits – where you have your "home." This means you know and feel these patterns of behavior are yours. You may feel like two summaries seem to describe you. All of the summaries may describe aspects of each of us.

Discernment is a process. Stay with it. It is your work but if it helps to ask someone close to you for help, in your discernment, that is fine. You may be feeling your wing style influence to your core personality type. Remember this is about your personality type and you are looking for your general patterns. Be as honest and vulnerable with yourself as possible. Your type will emerge soon enough.

One tip that may help: If you feel that you are a heart-centered person, one who likes and seeks the approval of others, and in stress can get drama going, it is likely you will be in this triad, either, Type Two, Loving Giver, Type Three, Effective Achiever, or Type Four, Original-Romantic.

If you feel that you are a head–centered type, and in stress you can overthink and get a monkey mind-set going, it is likely you will be in this triad: Type Five, Wise Observer, Type Six, Loyal Skeptic, or Type Seven, Joyful Adventurer.

If you feel that you can get over-reactive, having "knee-jerk reactions" in stress, it is likely you could be either Type 8 Powerful Protector, Type 9 Peaceful Mediator, or Type 1, Good Reformer.

Another helpful general insight in discerning type comes from Karen Horney, (1885-1952) Enneagram Author, "Our Inner Conflicts," (1945.) She teaches us that Types Three, Seven and Eight are "move against – go for it" types and Type Four, Five and Nine are "move away from – withdrawing" types, and Type One, Two and Six are "move towards – dutiful" types.

Read the nine summaries that follow:

A. People have told me that I am intense, a dreamer, and dramatic. I feel things deeply, sometimes it seems as though I feel them more deeply than others. I long for and dream about things to make it all seem better.

I can get sad when I cannot make these things happen, and then it seems like I am often wanting what I cannot have. It sounds like I am a victim, but I feel alone much of the time, or at least when I am down. I long for happiness and the deep connection with others, yet I seem cut off somehow. Sometimes it seems

162

that others have it so much better than I do. I feel good when I move my desires or yearnings into action, and yet when I am unable to do this, I guess I get overly dependent on others or I seek their approval too much.

B. I am told I am mellow, or laid back, or easygoing. I like to see all sides of an issue and when I am stressed, it is tough for me to differentiate, or discriminate between this way or that way, as being "the right way". When stressed, I see a lot of "shades of grey," in my thinking and feeling.

I do not know what I want sometimes and so I just go along and try to get along with what others want. I say things like "whatever" or "it doesn't matter to me." If I do not resolve things, I feel that they will just work themselves out most of the time. Sometimes I go on and on like this passively and then out of the blue, I will get very angry. People close to me might also say I'm passive-aggressive. I guess I can live vicariously through others.

C. I am like the rabbit in the yard. I watch closely and can worry about things. I can also be like a dog or snake who bites when he is fearful, lashing out at others when I am experiencing a lot of doubt or fear.

I can sense if people are trustworthy or not, and when I feel safe, I can hear my inner voice very strongly, and can be very true to myself. I can also be very true to my friends or close associates, if they prove themselves to be trustworthy.

When something is more familiar or when it is within my realm of comfort, I do not have as much of a problem being suspicious of it. It is when things get too different from what I am used to that my ears can perk up, and I can distrust easily. I often ask, "What is the worst thing that can happen?" hoping to get that out of the way so I can get on with things.

The world can be threatening; I guess I could be more open to and positive about all the options that are available.

D. I like to take charge and have no problem leading a group. I like to be direct, and say what I mean and mean what I say and want others to do the same. I do not like games that people can play. If I don't respect you, you cannot be my authority. If someone acts weak, or helpless, it can really bother me. It especially bothers me if they act like victims of their situation. Sometimes people say I get loud, bossy and controlling, but I step in when I feel it is necessary. I know how to protect the underdog too. I don't understand why people would want to hurt someone, and I can stand up for people who are being treated unfairly. I like feeling my strength and the strength of others. I could feel my softer side more often.

E. I am a people person. People tell me that I am caring, or helpful, and I get so much pleasure out of making people happy. People have told me I know what they need before they do, or at least I can sense what it is they are needing. I will give a lot in my relationships but when I feel that people do not want to give back to me, I can become very resentful, even vindictive. After all, I do a lot for them and I feel it should be reciprocated.

Because I have been taught giving is better than receiving, I often avoid my own desires, or become anxious asking people what they might do for me. Sometimes I don't even know what it is I truly need. Other people's needs seem easier to figure out than my own. I could pay myself first more often.

F. I always see a way to make things better. It is sometimes hard for me to see things that are incorrect or could be done better, even if it is not my problem. Some people tell me to not be so rigid or they tell me to get off my "high horse."

I can be demanding, but I have strong principles. If I see something is wrong, I feel I need to speak up about it. I certainly have high expectations for myself. In fact, I have a critical streak that can be hard to live with. If I don't do something right, I can beat myself up. Then I can get down on myself for beating myself up. That feels like spinning my wheels. I know how to have fun too but I am very serious, really. I am a hard worker and very dependable. If I give you my word you can count on me to come through. I wish I could lighten up.

G. I don't like mistakes or laziness. I like to "walk the talk." I am very capable, even driven and competitive, and I like being a good team leader. Delegating can be hard for me, especially if the person to whom I am delegating doesn't share my drive or love of success. In all my roles, I work to be the best, to be a success. There is always a lot to do in my eyes. "No rest for the wicked," they say. People tell me I am quick and impatient at times, and they often tell me I am ambitious or I get a lot done. The roles I play and image I present often have a great sense of urgency and are very important to me. I do not like to whine about overworking and would rather just get the job done. When I get depleted, I zone out, numb myself out with screens or food, drink or I collapse. It might help me to not focus so much about my role or image and let my real feelings count more often.

H. I like to be alone and not have to deal with a lot of people. "My cave" is comforting to me, and often where you will find me, alone or maybe with one person. People close to me have told me I can be off-putting or withholding. It can be difficult for me when people want me to share their problems or feelings. I actually can listen to their feelings easier than I can share my own. I don't even know what my deep feelings are a lot of the time. I like to see the big picture, and analyze things so I can understand it thoroughly and I am often told that I am bright or smart. Learning and collecting new data is appealing for me. It isn't that I don't like people, I do, but it just seems more fun sometimes thinking about them after we have been together. I'm not really a party or people person, and sometimes I can come across as aloof. When sharing feelings with people, I need to know people well, and that takes time. I could reach out more and share.

I. I am pretty grateful for everything I have. I think life should be fun and we all shouldn't be so serious so often. There is always something that I can find interesting and get involved in, so I can get distracted, or scattered. I am an optimist, and like to be in gratitude. I often have a lot of energy for whatever it is that I am into. I always see the glass half full, and while people seem to like that about me, I drive some people crazy because I can jump around when we talk. They might not see how it relates to the topic but I do. Or, they tell me I'm funny. I like to see the big picture of things, and often wonder about it all. When things are limiting or emotionally painful, I like to think of happy things. If it is a tough day or week, making plans, and having something to look forward will give me a lift. I would like to be more focused but I actually am good at a lot of things.

Answers to the quiz are on following page...

Answers to Enneagram Quiz

Which number are you? Match the numbers to their counterpart summaries above.

A-4, B-9, C-6, D-8, E-2, F-1, G-3, H-5, I-7

APPENDIX B:

Enneagram Types And Their "Songs" (My Choice)

Type One, the Good Reformer
It's time to see what I can do—to test the limits and break through—no right no wrong no rules for me, I'm free. Let it go, let it go, the perfect boy is gone.
LET IT GO, Disney movie, FROZEN

Type Two, the Loving Giver
Lean on me, when you're not strong, and I'll be your friend. I'll help you carry on, for it won't be long, when I'm gonna need somebody to lean on.
LEAN ON ME by Bill Withers

Type Three, the Effective Achiever
Say you don't need no diamond ring, and I'll be satisfied. Tell me that you want the kind of things that money just can't buy. Money can't buy me love.
MONEY CAN'T BUY ME LOVE by Lennon-McCartney

Type Four, the Original, Romantic

You may say I'm a dreamer but I'm not the only one. I hope someday you'll join us, and the world will live as ONE.
IMAGINE by John Lennon

Type Five, the Wise Observer

Even if your hands are shaking and your faith is broken. Even as the eyes are closing, do it with a heart wide open. Say what you need to say.
SAY by John Mayer

Type Six, the Loyal Skeptic

Got to step out on faith; it's time to show my face. Procrastination had me down. Look what I've found. Strength, courage and wisdom, it's been inside me all along.
STRENGTH, COURAGE AND WISDOM by India Arie

Type Seven, the Joyful Adventurer

I see trees of green, red roses too. A bright blessed world for me and you, and I think to myself, what a wonderful world.
WHAT A WONDERFUL WORLD by Louis Armstrong

Type Eight, the Powerful Protector

I believe that children are our future. Teach them well and let them lead the way. Show them all the beauty they possess inside, give them a sense of pride; let the children's laughter remind us of how we used to be.
GREATEST LOVE OF ALL by Whitney Houston

Type Nine, the Peaceful Mediator

It's not easy being green, having to spend each day blending with the color of the leaves, when I think it could be nicer being red or yellow or gold or something much more colorful like that.
IT'S NOT EASY BEING GREEN by Kermit the Frog, Best of Muppets

ABOUT THE AUTHOR

 Rosemary Hurwitz is a married mom of four young adults. Committed to a rich inner life, she found a way to cultivate it with the Enneagram, a practice she learned while in an MA, Pastoral Studies program at Loyola University in Chicago. Since 2001 when she received her Enneagram Certification, she has given workshops, classes and private Life Coaching sessions with this time-honored tool.

Rosemary says "It is among my greatest joys, to guide people to live a life where they are centered, safe and empowered. Turning on the light of their unique essence is an honor." Along with her husband, Dale, she also facilitated Discovery weekend retreats, a program for engaged couples patterned after Marriage Encounter for twenty-five years. Rosemary is Co-author of *No Mistakes: How You Can Change Adversity into Abundance*, *(Hierophant Publishing, 2013), 365 Days of Angel Prayers, and 111 Morning Meditations(2015, 2017, SDJ Productions). Who You Are Meant To be, The Enneagram Effect*, is her first book. Rosemary is on the faculty at Common Ground in north suburban Chicago as well as other Educational and Holistic centers. Visit her at www.spiritdrivenliving.com

ACKNOWLEDGMENTS

Thank you to Shanda Trofe of Transcendent Publishing for her professionalism, dedication and kindness!

To Dana Micheli and Carol Doody, my Editors, for your patience, kindness and ability to help me be clear, I thank you! Your faith in this subject and in me along with your editing skills are most appreciated!

To my family of origin, my poetry-writing mom Rose and Communications Author and dad, Joe (in heaven), I am so grateful for you. To my siblings and their spouses, Lynn, Jane and George, Ann (and Steve in heaven,) Joanie (in heaven) and Mike, and Michael and Holly, thank you all for believing in and challenging me to my personal best.

G. Gilbert said: "Families are mirrors of our past, present and future." It is true, and I love you all and always will.

Love and gratitude to my mother-in-law Minnette, and her spouse Rex (in heaven) and father-in-law Buddy. Dale's sisters and our brother-in-laws, Leslie and Greg, Jamie, and John and Marla and Tom.

To my forever friends; Diane Strobel, Cathy Anthony and Donna Friedeck, Nancy Doherty and Beth Bagg. You are like sisters to me. How graced we have been to share this journey together.

To Dr. John Bond, my spiritual father on earth, my deepest thanks for helping me with my connection to my spirit and my wholeness at the fragile beginning of my adulthood. With you, I found such a great foundation for my personal and spiritual growth.

To Dr. Donna Amstutz, you are a *Madonna* who showed me how to strengthen and protect myself by always directing me to the safety within. You helped me be the best partner and mother I could be, by first being a loving and intuitive partner and mother to myself.

To our dear Discovery friends, for all Dale and I have learned in service with you to the engaged couples who shared our retreats. Special thanks to Carol and Dan, Meg and Dan, Joe and Joanne, Bob and Dolores, Joanne and Tom, and Nick and Hilary for sharing this beautiful gift of discovery within ourselves and our marriages.

To Dr. Ron Miller (in heaven) Spiritual Author, favorite teacher, Chair of Religion at Lake Forest College, Co-founder of Common Ground: Thank you for noticing me, believing in me, giving retreats with me, and mentoring me in this life-giving career of Spiritual Teacher and Coach.

To Jim Kenney, Director and Co-founder of Common Ground, for the honor of working with you on Common Ground faculty and for the wonderful mission we share.

Big thanks to authors and friends who have encouraged me in the Enneagram and Holistic field. There have been so many that have inspired me, especially, Dr. Jerry Wagner, Dr. Helen Palmer and Dr. David Daniels

To Caroline Myss, Neale Donald Walsh, and Marianne Williamson. don Miguel Ruiz, Jr., Sonia Choquette, the late Debbie Ford and the late Wayne Dyer, The many classes and retreats with you as mentors have graced my life. At a writer's retreat, Wayne told me not to worry about when this book got written, even if it was in another lifetime, it would come in when it was needed – I loved that! Sonia, you told me I would write a book and here it is!

A special thanks to Jerry Wagner for your great teaching on the Enneagram and willingness to help in my career. To Darren Weissman, for your wonderful friendship, faith in me and in my midlife career change, offering me my first job in your office, giving private Enneagram-based-coaching sessions. You walk in the ways of wholeness, and inspire me to do the same- infinite love and gratitude for you..

To Susan Opeka, founder of The Present Moment, for your belief in my work, the many opportunities that come from The Present Moment, and your dear friendship.

To Randy Davilla, my publisher for *"No Mistakes, How You Can Change Adversity into Abundance,"* and Caroline Pincus, editor, who encouraged me early on. Thank you, Randy, for this book's subtitle and for all your advice, sensitivity combined with straight talk, and skills.

Special thanks to Sunny Dawn Johnston for reaching out to me in Co-Authoring several inspirational projects, 365 Days of Angel Prayers and more, and for your belief in me.

Last, never least, to my students, private clients and readers: Congratulations! It takes courage to do this inner work but it's so worth it. I am wildly grateful that you cared enough to look within and be decidedly more resourceful within each new day. I am right alongside you!

Made in the USA
Columbia, SC
06 January 2021